I0755426

JACOB TENDING THE FLOCKS OF LABAN.

LINE UPON LINE;

OR

A SECOND SERIES

OF THE

EARLIEST RELIGIOUS INSTRUCTION

THE

INFANT MIND IS CAPABLE OF RECEIVING

WITH

VERSES ILLUSTRATIVE OF THE SUBJECTS.

BY THE AUTHOR
OF THE "PEEP OF DAY."

Line upon line, line upon line; here a little and there a little.—ISA. 28 : 10.

PUBLISHED BY THE
AMERICAN TRACT SOCIETY,
150 NASSAU-STREET, NEW YORK.

PREFACE.

The design of this little work is to lead children to understand, and to delight in the Scriptures.

If adults meet with difficulties in the sacred text, which commentaries often remove, children must necessarily meet with many more, some of which this little book may clear up. Since it is evident that commentaries would not suit the volatile minds of children, however simply they might be written, some other kind of help ought to be provided for them. The best assistance would no doubt be afforded by the parent's voice: for no book can so forcibly arrest the attention, or touch the heart, as the remarks of a tender parent. But where children do not enjoy this advantage, a book may in some measure supply its place; and where they do possess it, may recall to mind parental instructions.

Many interesting histories have been omitted, because the writer feared to swell the size of the work, and judged it better to relate the principal events in detail than to give an abridged account of all.

But it is intended that these omissions should be supplied, (if the Lord will,) and that shortly the history of Job should be published, and subsequently that of the Judges, and of the kings of Israel and Judah.

CONTENTS.

LINE UPON LINE.

CHAPTER I.*

THE CREATION.

Gen. i.

My dear children,—I know that you have heard that God made the world. Could a man have made the world? No; a man could not make such a world as this.

Men can make many things, such as boxes and baskets. Perhaps you know a man who can make a box. Suppose you were to shut him up in a room, which was quite empty, and you were to say to him, "You shall not come out till you have made a box,"—would the man ever come out? No—never. A man could not make a box, except he had something to make it of. He must

* The teacher will generally find the proof of every statement, either in the chapters of the Bible referred to at the beginning of each chapter in this book, or in the notes affixed; but in the opening of this work the proofs are often withheld, because they have already been given in those parts of the "Peep of Day" in which the same subjects are treated.

have some wood, or some tin, or some pasteboard, or some other thing. But God had nothing to make the world of. He only spoke, and it was made.*

Making things of nothing, is called "creating." No one can create anything, but God.†

Do you know why God is called the Creator? It is because he created all things. There is only one Creator. Angels cannot create things, nor can men. They could not create one drop of water, or one little fly.

You know that God was six days in creating the world. I will tell you what he did on each day.

I.

On the first day, God said, "Let there be light;" and there was light.

II.

On the second day, God spoke again, and there was water very high; that water is called the clouds. There was also water very low. There was nothing but water to be seen. God filled every place with air; but you know the air cannot be seen.

III.

On the third day, God spoke, and the dry land appeared from under the water; and the water ran

* Things which are seen were not made of things that do appear.—Heb. xi. 3.

† Thou hast created *all* things.—Rev. iv. 11.

down into one deep place that God had prepared.* God called the dry land Earth, and he called the water Seas. We walk upon the dry land. We cannot walk upon the sea. The sea is always rolling up and down; but it can never come out of the great place where God has put it. God spoke, and things grew out of the earth. Can you tell me what things grew out of the earth? Grass, and corn, and trees, and flowers.

IV.

On the fourth day God spoke, and the sun and moon and stars were made. God ordered the sun to come every morning, and to go away in the evening,† because God did not choose that it should be always light. It is best that it should be dark at night, when we are asleep. But God lets the moon shine in the night, and the stars also; so that if we go out in the night, we often have a little light. There are more stars than we can count.

V.

On the fifth day, God began to make things that are alive. He spoke, and the water was filled with fishes, and birds flew out of the water, and perched upon the trees.

VI.

On the sixth day, God spoke, and the beasts came out of the earth: lions, sheep, cows, horses,

* Who shut the sea with doors, and brake up for it my decreed place?—Job. xxxviii. 8, 10.

† The sun knoweth his going down.—Ps. civ. 19.

and all kinds of beasts came out of the earth, as well as all kinds of creeping things, such as bees, ants, and worms, which creep upon the earth.

At last, God made a man. God said, "Let us make man in our likeness."* To whom did God speak? To his Son, the Lord Jesus Christ: his Son was with him when he made the world. God made man's body of the dust, and then breathed into him. The man had a soul as well as a body. So the man could think of God. Afterwards God made the woman of a piece of the flesh and bone from the man's side, as you have heard before.

God gave all the other creatures to Adam and Eve; and he blessed them, and put them into the garden of Eden, and desired Adam to take care of the garden.

When God had finished all his works, he saw that they were very good. He was pleased with the things he had made. They were all very beautiful. The light was glorious; the air was sweet; the earth was lovely, clothed in green; the sun and moon shone brightly in the heavens; the birds, and beasts, and all the living creatures, were good and happy, and Adam and Eve were the best of all, for they could think of God, and praise him.

VII.

You know there are seven days in the week. Now, on the seventh day, God did not make any-

* In the beginning was the word; and the word was with God and the word was God. All things were made by him—John i. 1. 3

thing; but he rested from all his works. He called the seventh day his own day, because he rested on it. This is the reason people rest on the seventh day, and call it God's day. It is the sabbath day. It is the great day for praising God.*

None of the creatures that God had made in the six days could praise him with their tongues, except Adam and Eve.

Angels in heaven can praise God, and men upon earth.

My little children, do you ever praise God? You have learned little hymns in his praise. Perhaps you know the hymn that begins,

> "And now another day is gone,
> I'll sing my Maker's praise."

Does God like to hear you praise him? Yes; when you think of him, and love him, while you are praising him.

Angels always praise God with their hearts, and so should we.

Let us now count the things that God made on each day:—

First day, Light.

Second day, Air and Clouds.

Third day, Earth and Sea, and the things that grow.

Fourth day, Sun, Moon, and Stars.

* I went with them to the house of God, with the voice of joy and *praise*, with a multitude that kept *holy day*.—Ps. xlii. 4.

Fifth day, Fishes and Birds.

Sixth day, Beasts and Creeping Things, and Man.

Seventh day, Nothing; God rested.

All things the mighty Lord,
Created by his word;
And all his creatures are,
From worm to brightest star;
His wonders none can imitate,
Or out of nothing can create.

Were angels to unite
Their heavenly skill and might,
How vainly they would try
To make one little fly!
For *life* they never could bestow,
Nor cause the meanest flower to grow.

Angels so fair and strong
Unto the Lord belong;
From him their beauty came;
'Tis he sustains their frame:
They could not live one single hour.
Unless supported by his power.

And this the angels know;
Around God's throne they bow,
And humbly they confess
Their own unworthiness;
And still the King of kings admire,
And praise him with their tongues of fire.

Far lower should *I* lie
Before the Lord most high;
For how can I compare
With angels strong and fair!
I who am made of sinful clay,
And like the grass must fade away?

CHAPTER II.

THE SIN OF ADAM.

Gen. iii.

You remember that God put Adam and Eve in a pretty garden. There they lived very happily. They never quarrelled with each other: they were never sick nor in pain. Adam worked in the sweet garden; but not so hard as to tire himself. His work was quite pleasant, for it was never too hot nor too cold in that sweet garden; and there were no weeds nor thistles growing in the ground.

You know there was one tree of which Adam might not eat. The name of the tree was "The tree of the knowledge of good and evil."

God had said, that if Adam ate of it, he should die. Adam and Eve might eat of all the other trees in the garden.

Do you not think that they had fruit enough without eating of the tree of knowledge of good and evil? They did not wish to eat of it, as God had told them not. They loved God. He was their friend, and used to walk and talk with them in the garden. Now you shall hear how Adam and Eve grew wicked.

You know that there are a great many wicked angels; one of them is called "Satan," and he is the prince of the wicked angels. Satan knew that if Adam and Eve grew wicked, they would die and go to hell. Satan hated them, and wished to make them unhappy; so he thought, "I will try and persuade them to eat that fruit which God has told them not to eat." So Satan put on the body of a serpent,* and came into the garden.

He saw Eve; he pretended to be kind, and said to her, "Why do you not eat of the fruit?"

But she said, "God has told us not to eat of that fruit, and that if we do, we shall die."

But the serpent said, "No; you shall not die; but this fruit will make you wise, like God."

The woman was afraid to eat; but she looked, and thought the fruit *nice;* she looked again, and thought it *pretty;*† and she thought "I should like to eat it." So she took the fruit and gave some to Adam.

Sad was that hour! no more happy days for Adam and Eve. They were grown naughty; they knew they had done wrong; they were afraid of seeing God. Soon they heard his voice in the garden; they went and hid themselves among the thick trees. They wished they had some clothes to cover them; but they had only some leaves that they sewed together.

God called Adam, and said, "Adam, where art thou?"

Then Adam said, "I was afraid, because I was naked, and I hid myself."

* That old serpent, called the Devil, and Satan, which deceiveth the whole world.—Rev. xii. 9.

† And when the woman saw that the tree was good for food, and that it was pleasant to the eyes, &c.—Gen. iii. 6.

Then God said, "Who told you that you were naked? have you eaten of that tree?"

Then Adam said, "The woman you gave me, to be with me, she gave me of the tree, and I did eat."

God said to the woman, "What is this that thou hast done?"

And she said, "The serpent deceived me, and I did eat."

God was angry with them all, but most of all with the serpent. God cursed him, and said, "You shall always crawl on the ground, and eat dust."

Then God said to the Woman, "You shall often be sick, and Adam shall be your master, and you must obey him."

And God said to Adam, "You shall work hard, and dig the ground; thorns and thistles shall grow; you shall have bread to eat; but you shall be obliged to work so hard that drops of sweat shall often stand upon your forehead; you shall be sad while you live, and at last you shall die; your body was made of dust, and it shall turn into dust again."

What sad punishments these were! How sad Adam and Eve must have felt when they heard them But this was not all; they were not allowed to stay in the pretty garden. God drove them out, and God would not let them come into the garden again; so he desired an angel with a fiery sword to stand near it; yet God showed his pity by giving them clothes made of skins of beasts. They had tried to make clothes of the leaves of the trees, but God gave them better clothes.

Where do you think the souls of Adam and Eve must go when their bodies were dead? To Satan? That was what Satan hoped. But the blessed Lord Jesus had promised his Father to come down and save Adam and Eve, and their children, from hell.

Adam and Eve knew that a child should one day be born, who should save people from going to hell.* So they had some comfort in their hearts, when they went out of the garden.

It was a long while before Jesus did make himself a little child, and did come into this world; but at last he came, and died upon the cross.

My little children, was it not very kind in Jesus to say that he would come and die for us?—ought we not to love him very much?

How pleasant once was Adam's toil
  In Eden's cool retreat!
But now he tills a thorny soil,
  And faints beneath the heat.

How lovely once (how altered now!)
  Were Adam's form and face!
Bright was that eye, and smooth that brow,
  Now clouded by disgrace.

* God said to the serpent, in the presence of Adam and Eve. "I will put enmity between thee and the woman, and between thy seed and her seed; it shall bruise thy head, and thou shalt bruise his heel." Gen. iii. 15.

His hair turns gray, his body stoops
  Beneath the weight of years;
And Eve with pain and sickness droops,
  And from her eyes flow tears.

Yet murmur not, O wretched pair,
  Against the Lord Most High,
He made you happy, good, and fair,
  And warn'd you not to die.

And now he kindly promises
  To wash your sins away,
And let you taste of happiness
  Which never shall decay.

This promise, too, will cost him dear;
  (But, Oh! his love is great;)
His only Son must suffer here,
  And die 'midst scorn and hate.

A sweeter paradise is won,
  Than you in Eden lost;
There God shines brighter than the sun,
  Amidst his heavenly host.

A few more years of suffering past,
  Your souls shall reach that shore;
Your bodies at the trumpet's blast,
  Shall rise to die no more.

CHAPTER III.

CAIN AND ABEL.

Gen. iv.

AFTER Adam and Eve were turned out of the garden, they had two little children; their names were Cain and Abel.

Cain was wicked like Satan; but Abel was good; for though he was naughty, yet God had given him his Holy Spirit, so that he loved God. Abel was sorry for his sins, and asked God to forgive him;* and God did forgive him.

Cain and Abel were obliged to work hard like Adam their father. Cain dug the ground, and planted trees, and reaped corn. Abel took care of sheep; he was a shepherd.

Now I will tell you how Cain and Abel behaved to God.

God did not walk and talk with people then, as he had done in the garden; but he did speak sometimes, and he allowed people to pray to him. You know that Jesus had promised to die for Adam and his children, and that was the reason that God was so kind to them.

God wished them always to remember that Jesus had promised to die for them; so he taught them a way of keeping it in their minds.

* *All* have sinned, and come short of the glory of God.—Rom. iii. 23. (By *faith*) the elders obtained a good report.—Heb. xi. 2.

He told them to heap up stones, (this heap was called an altar,) and then to put some wood upon the altar; and to take a lamb, or a kid, and to bind it with a rope to the altar; then to take a knife and to kill the lamb; and then to burn it on the altar. Doing this, was called "offering a sacrifice."

When people did this, God wished them to think how he would one day let his Son die for their sins.* When Jesus was nailed to the cross, he was like a lamb tied to the altar.†

Abel brought lambs, and offered them up to God; and Abel thought of God's promise, so God was pleased with Abel, and with his sacrifice. But Cain did not obey God, but brought some fruit, instead of a lamb; and so God was angry with Cain and did not like his sacrifice.

Then Cain was very angry, and hated Abel, because he was good, and because God loved him best. Cain was envious of Abel.

Then God spoke to Cain, and said, "Why are you angry? If you will love and serve me, I shall be pleased with you; but if not, you shall be punished."

Still Cain went on in wickedness. Now hear what he did at last.—One day he was talking with Abel in a field, when he rose up and killed him.

* By *faith*, Abel offered unto God a more excellent sacrifice than Cain—Heb. xi. 4.

† Behold the Lamb of God, which taketh away the sins of the world John i. 29.

Abel's blood was spilt upon the ground. Abel was the first man that ever died. So Cain began by hating Abel, and ended by killing him though he was his brother·

Soon Cain heard the voice of God calling him; God said, "Where is your brother Abel?"

"I know not," answered wicked Cain; "am I my brother's keeper?"

But God said, "I have seen your brother's blood upon the ground; and you are cursed. You shall leave your father and mother, and wander about on the earth."

Cain said, "My punishment is greater than I can bear. O let me not be killed!"

God said, "You shall not be killed; but you shall wander about from place to place."

So Cain went and lived a great way off, and built houses for himself and his children. They lived in wickedness; they were the children of the devil, and cared not for God.

So Adam and Eve lost both their sons in one day; for Cain went a great way off, and Abel died. How they must have wept as they put dear Abel in the ground! But they must have wept still more to think that Cain was so wicked.

Why did they eat the fruit when Satan bade them? If they had not eaten the fruit, they would never have been unhappy: Cain would not have been wicked, and Abel would not have died. But God had pity on Adam and Eve, and gave them another son, who was made good by God's Spirit: he was called Seth.

The children of Seth feared God; and God loved them and called them his children.

Cain was the babe the first on earth
  Rejoic'd a mother's sight:
Now Eve laments the infant's birth,
  Once hail'd with fond delight.

O how could she foresee the day,
  When she beheld her child,
As wrapt in slumbers soft he lay,
  Or playfully he smiled!

But though so lovely to the view,
  Evil lay hid within;
And Satan watch'd him, as he grew,
  And fann'd the sparks of sin.

At length Cain shed his brother's blood
  Then sought the deed to hide;
Now banish'd from his parents' God,
  He wanders far and wide.

CHILD.

Guard me, O Lord from Satan's power,
  For he walks to and fro,
And like a lion would devour
  The souls of men below.

Pride, hate, and envy, are the chains,
  By which he holds them fast;
Nor let them know what bitter pains
  Their sins shall bring at last.

CHAPTER IV.

THE FLOOD.

CAIN had a great many children; Seth had a great many children.

At last Adam and Eve died, and Cain died, and Seth died; but still there were a great many people in the world. Were the people good or wicked?

At first some were good, but at last they all grew wicked, except one man: his name was Noah.* The spirit of God was in his heart, and he loved God.

God was very angry with the wicked people, and he determined to punish them.

God said to Noah, "I will make it rain so much that all people shall be drowned, except you, and your wife, and your children."

Then God told Noah to make a great ark.

What is an ark? It is like a boat, or a ship. Noah made a very great ark, which would swim upon the top of the water, when God should drown the wicked people.

Noah made the ark of wood. Noah cut down many trees, and cut boards, and fastened them together. He made one door in the ark, and one little window at the top.

Noah told the people that God was going to

* Noah, a preacher of righteousness.—2 Peter. ii. 5.

drown the world and advised them to leave off their wickedness.

But they would not mind. Still they went on eating and drinking, and not thinking of God, noı trying to please him.*

God did not choose that all the beasts, and birds, and insects should be drowned; so he desired No ah to get some birds of every sort, and some beasts of every sort, and some insects of every sort, and to bring them into the ark. God could make all these animals go quietly in the ark. Noah put corn, and fruit, and grass into the ark for them to eat when they were in the ark.

So Noah got some birds of every sort; some doves, some ravens, some eagles, some sparrows, some larks, some goldfinches, and many others, and they flew in at the window. Noah got some beasts of every kind, some sheep, some horses, some dogs: and he got some insects of every kind; some butterflies, some ants, some bees.

All these went into the ark; for God made them gentle and obedient. Then Noah himself went in with his wife, his three sons, and their wives. How many people where there in the ark?—eight people. But Noah did not shut the door: God shut the door, and Noah knew that he must not open it till God bade him.

Then it began to rain. It rained all day and

* They did eat, they drank, they married wives, they were given in marriage until the day that Noah entered into the ark, and the flood came and destroyed them all.—Luke xvii. 27.

all night. What did the wicked people think now? How they must have wished that they had minded Noah! If they climbed trees, the water soon reached to the tops; if they went up high mountains, as high as the clouds, the water rose as high as they; for it rained forty days and forty nights. All beasts and birds, and men, and children died, except those that were in the ark.

At last nothing was to be seen but water, and the ark floating upon the top of the water. How long did Noah live in the ark? Almost one whole year.

A long while after it had left off raining, Noah wished to know whether the waters were dried up. He went among his birds, and chose a raven, and let it out of the window. A raven is a fierce bird. It did not like the ark; though there were no trees to be seen, nothing but water, yet the raven would not go back to Noah, but went on flying night and day over the water.

When Noah saw that the raven did not come back, he went among his birds, and chose a dove. A dove is a very gentle bird. Noah put it out at the window; and when it saw nothing but water, the dove came back to the ark. Noah knew when his bird came back, (perhaps it pecked at the window,) and he put out his hand and pulled it in.

Noah waited seven days, then Noah sent the dove out again; and this time the dove saw some trees: yet the dove did not stay, but plucked off a leaf with its beak, and came back to Noah. Noah must have loved his good little dove.

Noah waited seven days more, and then he sent out the dove again, and this time it did not come back. Now Noah knew that the earth was dry, but he waited in the ark till God told him to go out.

At last God said, "Go out of the ark, you and your wife, your three sons, and their wives, and the birds, and the beasts, and the insects, and all the creeping things."

When the door was open, the beasts came out. How glad the sheep must have been to lie down again upon the soft grass, and the goats to climb the high hills!

When the window was open, the birds flew out. How glad they must have been to perch again among the trees!

Noah saw all the green hills and fields again; but where were all the wicked people? he would never see their faces again.

Noah remembered God's goodness in saving him from being drowned. He made a heap of stones for an altar; he took some beasts and birds, and offered a sacrifice to God. God was pleased with this sacrifice.

Then God made a very kind promise to Noah. He said, "I will never drown the world again. When it rains, do not think there will be a flood. Look up in the sky after the rain, and you will see a bow. That shall be the sign that I remember my promise."

Have you seen a rainbow, dear children? How large it is! What beautiful colours it has! It puts us in mind of God's kind promise not to drown the world any more.

You know why God made this kind promise. It was because the Lord Jesus had promised one day to die for people's sins.

At last Jesus did come down and die: and one day he will come again, and then he will burn the world. I hope we shall then be saved as Noah was; but if God should find us caring only for eating and drinking, and playing, and not trying to please him, we shall be burnt up.*

O tell me how the nations passed
  The day before the flood:
O! did they know it was the last?
  And did they call on God?

    In merriment
    Their time is spent;
    They sing and play,
    And dance away;
    They eat and drink,
    And little think
They stand on endless ruin's brink.

    Some rear the walls
    Of sumptuous halls;

* Take heed to yourselves, lest at any time your hearts be overcharged with surfeiting, drunkenness, and *cares of this life*, and so that day come upon you unawares.—Luke xxi. 34.

Some join their hands
In marriage bands;
Some sell and buy;
All vainly try
To flee from God's all-seeing eye.

But God no more will silence keep;
He pours his wrath from high,
Unlocks the fountains of the deep,
And windows of the sky.

The clattering rain
Descends amain:
The rivers roar,
The torrents pour;
The waters rise
Till piteous cries
No more are heard beneath the skies.

At first, in flocks,
Men climb the rocks;
Nor fear to creep
Up mountains steep;
But waters flow
Where'er they go,
And wash them to the depths below.

Behold just Noah safely ride
Upon the mighty deep;
While all who once God's word defied.
Beneath the waters sleep.

CHILD.

Sudden as that tremendous day,
The judgment hour shall come;
Thousands shall then be swept away.
And meet an awful doom,

Let me not count these words a dream
And still refuse to hear;

However far the time may seem,
  Each hour it draws more near.

When once the fire begins to burn,
  'Twill be too late to pray;
Now from my cry God will not turn
  His gracious ear away.

CHAPTER V.

ABRAHAM, OR THE PROMISED LAND.

Gen. xii. 1—9.

NOAH'S sons had many children, and they had many children, and at last there were a great many people in the world. Were these people good or bad? They were bad. They did one very wicked thing. They cut down trees, and made the wood into little images, like dolls; then stuck them up and kneeled down and prayed to the images and said, "These images are our gods; they made us, and they gave us food to eat." These images were called *idols.*

Most of the people in the world worshipped idols, instead of the true God. Sometimes the idols were made of wood, sometimes of stone, or silver, or gold,

How glad I am, my dear children, that your mothers did not teach you to pray to idols! When you first could speak, they told you about the true God, and taught you to pray to him.

God looked down from heaven, and saw the people worshipping idols, and God was very angry.* But he did not kill them all, because Jesus had said he would die for the sins of men.†

Then God said, "I will choose one man, and teach him to love me, and to be my servant."‡ Now there was a man called Abraham. His father and his friends worshipped idols. God said to Abraham, "Leave your own home and your own friends and go to a country which I will show you, and I will bless you and take care of you.

Abraham did not know where God would tell him to go,‖ yet Abraham went because God told him to go. Abraham was obedient.

Abraham had a wife, called Sarah, whom he loved very much. Sarah went with Abraham. Abraham took some sheep, and cows, and asses with him, and some servants, who drove them and fed them.

But where could Abraham sleep at night?

* The wrath of God is revealed from heaven against *all* ungodliness. They are without excuse ; because that, when they knew God, they glorified him not as God.—Rom. i. 18, 20, 21.

† I will give thee for a light to the Gentiles ; that thou mayest be my salvation unto the end of the earth.—Isa. xlix. 6.

And the times of this ignorance God winked at ; but now commandeth all men everywhere to repent.—Acts xvii. 30.

‡ Who *raised* up the righteous man from the east, *called* him to his foot.—Isa. xli. 2.

Your fathers dwelt on the other side of the flood in old time, even Terah, the father of Abraham, &c. ; and they *served other gods.*—Josh xxiv. 2.

Thou art the Lord, the God, who didst *choose* Abram.—Neh. ix. 7.

‖ (Abraham) went out not *knowing whither* he went.—Heb. xi. 8.

There were very few houses to be seen; only fields and trees. Abraham slept in a tent. He made the tent with long sticks, and covered it over with skins of beasts.

Abraham could move his tent from place to place; for he had to travel a great many miles over high hills and wide rivers. At last he came to a beautiful country, full of trees and flowers and grass and corn. This was the place that God chose Abraham should live in. This place was called Canaan.

Abraham still lived in a tent. Sometimes he made a heap of stones, called an altar, and offered sacrifices of beasts to God. Abraham never worshipped idols; but all the people in Canaan did.

God often spoke to Abraham, and said, "I will bless you, and take care of you, and no one shall hurt you." God was pleased that Abraham had left his own home when he told him; and God called him his friend.*

Dear children: I hope that you will be like Abraham, and that you will mind what God says in the Bible. God has not told you to leave your home; but he has told you to be good and gentle, to speak the truth, and to love him, and he has promised to take you to heaven. If you obey God, he will call you his friend.† How pleasant to be God's friend?

* (Abraham was called the friend of God.—James ii. 23.

† Ye are my friends, if ye do whatsoever I command you.—John xv. 14.

Blest was the choice that Abraham made,
When he the voice of God obey'd,
  And left his kindred dear.
What though he knew not where he went
And passed his days within a tent,
  He knew that God was near.

And when he saw the heathen round,
Beneath each tree, upon each mound,
  Before their idols, bend,
Could he enough his love express
For Him who promised still to bless,
  And chose him for his friend?

The friend of God!—The angels fair
No sweeter name than this could bear,
  However high their state;
Yet many a creature, made of clay,
Who will the Lord's commands obey,
  Obtains this honour great.*

CHAPTER VI.

ABRAHAM, OR THE PROMISED CHILD.

Gen. xv.; xviii. 1—22; xxi. 1—6.

ABRAHAM and Sarah lived in a tent in the land of Canaan. They had no little child. Abraham was a very old man, and Sarah was a very old woman. They were both much older than your grandfather and grandmother. Abraham was al-

* Ye are my friends, if ye do whatsoever I command you.—John xv. 14.

most one hundred years old, and Sarah was almost ninety.

One night God said to Abraham. "Come out of your tent, and look up to the sky. What do you see?"

The sky was full of stars, more than could be counted. And God said, "You shall have a great many grandchildren and great-grandchildren, and they shall have more children, and they shall have more children, till there are as many people as there are stars in the sky: and they shall live in the land of Canaan, and the wicked people shall be turned out of it."

Now Abraham had not even *one* little child; yet he believed that God would do as he had promised. It was very right in Abraham to believe all that God said; for God always speaks the truth, and keeps his word.

One day, Abraham was sitting in his tent. It was about twelve o'clock in the day, and it was very hot indeed, but the tent was under a tree. Abraham looked up, and he saw three men a little way off. He ran to meet them, and bowed down, and said to one of the men, "My lord, pray come and rest yourself, and let me bring a little water to wash your feet, and a little bread for you to eat, and then you can go on your journey." And the men said that they would rest themselves.

Who do you think these men were? They were angels, though they looked like men. They had come from heaven with a message from God to Abraham. For you know that God sends his angels on messages to men. Angels are often near us, though we cannot see them.

The angels sat outside the tent under the shade of the tree. Sarah was in the tent. Abraham said to Sarah, "Take some flour, and make some cakes, and bake them very quickly." Then Abraham ran to his cattle, and took a fat calf, and said to one of his servants, "Kill it, and roast it quickly."

When it was ready, Abraham brought some butter, and some milk, and the cakes and the calf, and spread the dinner under the tree. The three men began to eat, and Abraham stood by them.

While they were eating, they said to Abraham, "Where is Sarah your wife?" And Abraham said, "She is in the tent." Then one of the men said, "Sarah, you shall have a son."

Sarah heard what the angel said, and she could not believe that she would *really* have a child now she was very old: so she laughed to herself.

The angel said, "Why did Sarah laugh? She shall certainly have a son." Then Sarah said, "I did not laugh;" for she was afraid. But the angel said, "You did laugh."

Then the three men got up, and went on farther. Abraham walked with them a little way, and then came back to his tent.

Do you think that God remembered his promise? The next year Sarah had a son. His name was Isaac. He was a good child, and God loved him.

Abraham and Sarah were much pleased with their little son.

So you see that God kept his promise. He had said that Abraham and Sarah should have a little son, and he gave them a son. It was right in Abraham to believe God's promise, and God too was pleased with Abraham for believing what he said.* Sarah did not believe at first: but she believed afterwards;† and God was pleased with her too.

My little children, you should believe all God's promises. What has God promised? To give you the Holy Spirit if you ask him. Do you believe his promise? Then pray to God to give you the Spirit. He will keep his promise; you may be sure that he will.

CHAPTER VII.

ABRAHAM, OR THE TRIAL OF LOVE.

Gen. xxii.

At last, Isaac grew up to be a man. He lived in a tent as Abraham and Sarah did. They all three loved God, and loved each other very much. It was a happy little family.

* (Abraham) staggered not at the promise of God through unbelief; but was strong in faith, giving glory to God; and being fully persuaded that what he had promised, he was able to perform: and therefore it was imputed to him for righteousness.—Rom. iv. 20—22.

† Heb. xi. 11.

Now you know that Abraham had a great many things. He had cows and asses, sheep and goats, tents and servants, silver and gold. But he had one thing that he loved more than these. What was that? His son, his dear son Isaac. He loved him more than anything else he had.

Yet there was one Being whom Abraham loved even better still. Who was that? God. Why ought Abraham to love God better than all? Because God had given him all he had.

At last, God said he would try Abraham, to see whether he loved him more than *anything* in the world: more even than he loved his son Isaac.

You have heard how Abraham used to burn lambs upon altars. Now God said to Abraham, "Take your dear son Isaac, and offer him up on an altar in a place that I will show.

Was not this a very hard thing for Abraham to do? But Abraham wished to do all God told him; because Abraham loved God so much. So Abraham cut down some wood to burn; he put the wood upon an ass, and he told two of his servants and Isaac to come with him. He left Sarah in the tent at home. They all four walked on for three days; at last they saw a high hill a great way off.

Abraham knew that was the place where he was to build the altar; so he said to his servants, "Stay here with the ass, while Isaac and I go and worship God on the top of the hill." He took the wood off the ass, and bound it round Isaac with a rope. Then he took some fire in one of his hands, and a knife in the other, and Abraham and Isaac walked up the hill together.

Isaac did not know that his father was going to offer him as a sacrifice; he thought that his father would offer a lamb. So he said, "Father." Abraham answered, "Here am I, my son." And Isaac said, "Here is fire and wood; but where is the lamb?" "My son," said Abraham, "God will find a lamb;" but Abraham did not tell Isaac that he was to be the lamb.

At last they came to the top of the hill. Then Abraham took stones, and built an altar; and he took the wood off Isaac's back, and laid it on the altar. Now the time was come, when Isaac must know who was to be the lamb. The rope that had bound the wood was fastened round the hands and feet of Isaac, and he was laid upon the wood like a lamb.

Then Abraham took the knife, and lifted up his hand to kill Isaac, when he heard a voice calling, "Abraham, Abraham." It was an angel speaking from heaven. The angel said, "Do not kill your son or hurt him at all; for now God knows that you love him, because you have given him your only son.

How glad was Abraham to untie the rope that bound Isaac, and to find that he need not kill him.

Abraham saw a ram caught in the bushes by the horns; and he went and took it, and offered it up as a sacrifice instead of Isaac. Abraham thanked

God very much for having given him back his son, and the angel called to him out of heaven again, and said, " God is much pleased with you for having given up your son; and God will bless you and all your children and grandchildren, and their children, and one of your children's children shall make all people happy."*

Whom did the angel mean? He meant that *Jesus would one day be* a child, and make people happy, and take them to heaven. A very long while afterwards, you know that Mary had a child, who was the Son of God.

When the angel had done speaking, Abraham and Isaac went down the hill together: there was no wood now on Isaac's back. Abraham now was very glad.

They found the servants where they had left them with the ass; then they all went back together to Sarah.

Are you quite sure that Abraham loved God? How do you *know* that he did? Because he obeyed God, and was ready to kill his son when God told him."†

Ought you to love God better than everything? Yes, you ought to love God best.

Why? Because God gave you everything.

* And now to Abraham and his *seed* were the promises made. He saith not, And to *seeds*, as of *many;* but as of *one*, And thy *seed* which is Christ. Gal. iii. 16.

† He that hath my commandments, and keepeth them, he it is that loveth me.—John xiv. 21.

That is one reason why you ought to love him best.

You love your father and mother very much: but you ought to love God better still. You ought to love God much better than you do your play, or your pretty things, or nice things to eat. Now, if you love God best you will do what he tells you.

You will not tell lies, for God tells you not; you will not fall in passions, and call people names: but you will try and please God. Then you will be like Abraham.

Ah! well may Abraham love the God
 Who promised him the land;
A thousand precious gifts bestowed,
 His warmest love demand.

His cattle cover o'er the plain,
 With gold his stores are fill'd;
His servants from a numerous train
 Prepared the sword to wield.

One gift, more precious than the rest,
 Does most his heart engage;
With a fair son is Abraham blest,
 The solace of his age.

Does he this son more fondly love
 Than his all-bounteous God?
This point the Lord would fully prove,
 So bids him shed his blood.

See Abraham labouring up the hill,
 With Isaac by his side;
The sorrows which his bosom fill,
 He strives awhile to hide.

And now the fatal altar's built,
And Abraham lifts the knife;
O! must his darling's blood be spilt
In the fair morn of life?

But hark! an angel stays his hand,
And bids him spare his son!
For he has done God's great command,
And faith and love has shown.

CHILD.

Like Abraham I am richly blest;
O! let me grateful be,
And ever love that God the best
Who gave so much to me.

O! let me his commands obey
With dutiful delight;
And, when he takes those gifts away,
Think all he does is right.

My God has done far more for me
Than can be e'er repaid;
His only son on Calvary
For me atonement made.

CHAPTER VIII.

JACOB, OR THE HEAVENLY DREAM.

Gen. xxiii. xxv. xxvii. xxviii.

ABRAHAM and Sarah were very, very old. At last Sarah died, and Abraham wished to bury her, but he had not a piece of ground in Canaan to bury her in; so he gave some of his silver to the people in Canaan, and bought a field.

The field was full of trees, and there was a cave in it. Abraham took the dead body of Sarah, and put it in the cave. At last Abraham died, and Isaac his son buried him in the same cave where Sarah lay.

Abraham will rise again out of that cave at the last day, and live with God in heaven. Abraham did not wish to have Canaan for his land; he wanted to live with God in heaven, which is a better country than Canaan.*

Abraham's spirit is not dead: it is with God now;† and at the last day his body will live too, and you will see him; and if you love God as Abraham did, you will sit down with Abraham in heaven.‡

Isaac married a good woman, called Rebekah. She lived in the tent where Sarah used to live.

Isaac and Rebekah had two little sons. They were called Esau and Jacob. They were twins; that is, they were the same age; but they were quite unlike each other. Their faces were unlike, and their hearts were unlike. Esau was wicked

* He looked for a city, which hath foundations, whose builder and maker is God.

Now they (the patriarchs) desired a better country, that is a heavenly.—Heb. xi. 10, 16.

† Now that the dead are raised, even Moses showed at the bush, when he called the Lord the God of Abraham, &c.; for he is not a God of the dead but of the living; for all live unto him.—Luke xx. 37. 38.

‡ Many shall come from the east and from the west, and shall *sit down with Abraham*, &c., in the kingdom of heaven.—Matt. viii 11.

from a child; but Jacob was good, and loved God. When Esau was a man he became a hunter. He had a bow and arrows; and he used to go into the woods, and shoot birds and stags; he used to bring them home, and dress them for dinner; and he used to give some of his nice meat to his father Isaac.

It was not wrong in Esau to hunt, and to cook the meat: but his heart was wicked: he did not care for God; and he loved meat and drink more than God.*

Jacob was a shepherd: he staid at home near his tent with his father and mother, and his sheep and goats. He loved God, and prayed to God very often.

I am sorry to tell you that Isaac loved wicked Esau better than he loved good Jacob. Shall I tell you why? Because Esau brought him nice meat. That was a very bad reason for loving him best.

But Rebekah loved Jacob, and God loved Jacob, and God did not love Esau.† Do you think that Esau and Jacob loved one another?

They did not; Jacob sometimes behaved unkindly to Esau; and Esau hated Jacob, and wished to kill him. One day Esau said, "My father will soon die; and then I will kill my brother Jacob."

* Lest there be any *profane* person as Esau, who for one morsel of meat sold his birth-right.—Heb. xii. 16.

† Jacob have I loved, but Esau have I hated. Rom. ix. 13.

Rebekah heard that Esau meant to kill Jacob some day ; so she was frightened, and called Jacob, and said to him, " Your brother Esau means to kill you. This is what you must do: go to your uncle, who lives a great way off, and stay with him. Soon Esau will leave off being angry ; then I will send for you home."

Jacob did as his mother advised. He took leave of his father Isaac, and Isaac blessed him before he went. Jacob did not ask his father to give him anything. He took no servant with him, no sheep, nor goats—not even an ass to ride upon. He only took a stick in his hand,* and he set out on his journey: Jacob felt very sad. He was a poor stranger, and he was going to a far country, which he had never seen.

Should not you feel very sad, if you were to leave your father and mother, and to go alone into a country a great way off?

He had no tent, nor house to sleep in by the way; so when night came, he took some stones for a pillow, and lay down to sleep on the ground. There were bears and wolves in that country; but God took care of him. God knew how sad he was; and God made him dream the sweetest dream that you ever heard.

In his sleep Jacob saw a great many steps reaching up to the sky; and on the steps beautiful angels; some going up, and some coming down: and at the top he saw God himself. Then Jacob

* With my *staff* I passed over this Jordan.—Gen. xxxii. 10.

heard a voice, and God spoke to him, and said, "I am the God of Abraham and of Isaac, and I will take care of you where ever you go: and I will bring you home again; and your children shall live in this land of Canaan, where you are sleeping."

Then Jacob awaked out of his sleep, but now his heart was glad; he knew that God and his angels were watching over him. He wished never to forget the place where he had this sweet dream: so he took the stones, which had been his pillow, and made them into a heap. "Now," he thought, "I shall be able to find the place, when God lets me come back to Canaan, as he has promised." He could not offer a sacrifice upon the stones, because he had no lambs, but he poured some oil upon them,* and he prayed to the Lord, and said, "If God will take care of me, and give me bread to eat, and clothes to wear, and bring me home again, he shall be my God, and this stone shall be God's house.

Jacob felt sure that God would take care of him, and bring him home again, because he had promised that he would.

God takes care of you, my dear children. He sends his angels down from heaven to watch over you, as they did over Jacob.

On the bare ground the traveller lies,
  The stones his pillow are;

* Jacob poured *oil* upon the top of the pillar.—Gen. xxvii. 18.

While slumbers close his weary eyes,
God sends a vision fair.

See on that wondrous airy way
What troops of angels move!
Their brightness turns the night to day,
Their faces beam with love.

And where the steps are lost in light
On heaven's glorious coast,
There stands the Lord, more wondrous bright,
Than that angelic host.

Like rushing waters loud and soft,*
Sounds the Almighty's voice,
Uttering sweet promises, which oft
Made Abraham's heart rejoice.

" Thy children shall this land possess,
(In number like the dust,)
And ONE all families shall bless,
Who place in him their trust.

" And I myself will go with thee,
Where'er thy footsteps roam;
Once more thy joyful eyes shall see
Thine own beloved home."

Sweet consolation thus is given
A wanderer's heart to cheer!
This house of God, this gate of heaven,
Shall be to memory dear.

CHILD.

And well I know that angels fair
E'en now from heaven *descend,*

I heard the noise of thy wings, like the noise of great *waters*, as the voice of the Almighty.—Ezek. i. 24.

That day and night they fill the air,
  And from all harm defend.*

And well I know that angels fair
  E'en now to heaven *ascend*,
And blest departed spirits bear†
  To their Almighty Friend.

And angels too shall guard *my* way,
  If I the Lord revere;
In life and death, by night and day,
  They still shall hover near.‡

CHAPTER IX.

JACOB, OR THE LONG JOURNEY.

Gen. xxix.

THEN Jacob went on his journey. He travelled for a great many days. At last he came to a place where there was a great deal of grass. In that place there was a well, and there was a great stone upon the top of the well. A great many sheep were round the well; and some men were with the sheep. These men were shepherds. There was very little water in that country where Jacob was. He must have been glad to have seen a well.

* Are they not all ministering spirts, sent forth to minister for them who shall be heirs of salvation?—Heb. i. 14.

† The beggar died and was carried by the angels into Abraham's bosom.—Luke xvi. 22.

‡ The angel of the Lord encampeth round about them that fear him, and delivereth them.—Ps. xxxiv. 7.

Jacob said to the shepherds, "Do you know a man called Laban?"--(that was the name of Jacob's uncle.)

"Yes," said they, "we do."

Then Jacob said, "Is he well?"

The shepherds answered, "He is well; and here is his daughter Rachael coming with the sheep."

Jacob was very glad to hear this, for Rachael was Jacob's cousin. He ran to her and kissed her, and he sobbed and wept.

Why did Jacob cry?

I think he cried for joy; for people sometimes cry for joy. Jacob had not seen a friend a long while, and he was glad to see his cousin.

Rachael did not know who Jacob was, till he said, "I am your cousin, and am come from a great way off."

Then Rachael ran, and said to her father Laban, "My cousin Jacob is come; I found him sitting by a well."

Then Laban was glad, and ran out to meet Jacob, and kissed him, and said, "You must come home to my house: I am your uncle."

Jacob told Laban that he would take care of his sheep; and so Jacob was Laban's servant. Jacob was a good shepherd, and sat up to guard the sheep at night from lions and bears. He cared not for the heat by day, nor the cold by night.*

* In the day the drought consumed me, and the frost by night; and my sleep departed from mine eyes.—Gen. xxxi. 40.

Laban had two daughters; one was called Leah, and the other Rachel; and Laban gave them to Jacob to be his wives. So Jacob had two wives. People must not have two wives now; but then they might have two wives, and even more than two.

God gave Jacob a great many little children. I *will not tell you* their names, because they were so many. Jacob lived a long while in some tents with his wives and his little children. He took care of Laban's sheep; but Laban gave him some sheep and goats of his own. Jacob had plenty of bread to eat and raiment to wear, as God had promised: for God always keeps his promises.

But Jacob could not forget his father and mother, and Canaan, where he had lived when he was a little boy. He knew that God had promised to give the land of Canaan to Abraham's, and Isaac's, and to his own children;* and he wished to live here again.

I will now write down the names of the good men who first lived in Canaan; and I will write down the names of their wives.

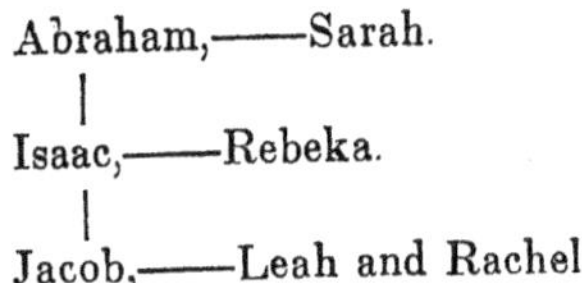

* By faith Abraham sojourned in the land of promise, as in a strange country, dwelling in tabernacles with Isaac and Jacob, *the heirs with him of the same promise.*—Heb. xi. 9.

The Lord has been poor Jacob's guide
Across the pathless desert wide,
And led him where his kindred dwell:
Lo! now he rests beside a well;
Its mouth is cover'd by a stone:
Around, the flocks are lying down.

For other flocks the shepherds stay,
Before they roll the stone away;
Jacob inquires their country's name;
It is the land whence Abraham came;
Behold fair Rachel leads her sheep,—
Why does the wanderer rise and weep?

In stranger lands his feet have stray'd
And now he weeps to see the maid,
Who of his mother's race is sprung,
Who speaks his own dear native tongue,
Who knows the God that he reveres;—
From *gladness* flow the wanderer's tears.

Now wipe those tears, and weep no more
For thee rich blessings lie in store;
The Lord is with thee, as he said,
Raiment provides, and daily bread;
With flocks and herds thy fields abound,
And lovely children sport around.

Nor will the Lord his promise break;
He ne'er will leave thee, nor forsake,
His power from harm will guard thy head,
And Canaan's land thy feet shall tread;
O Jacob's God! the faithful, true,
Be thou *my* God, and bless me too.

CHAPTER X.

JACOB, OR THE MEETING.

Gen. xxxi. xxxii. xxxiii. xxxv. 1—7.

At last Jacob said to Laban his uncle, " I have been your servant a long while, and now I want to go home." But Laban would not let Jacob go away; and he behaved very unkindly to Jacob; so that Jacob wished more and more to go home.

Once, while Jacob was taking care of the sheep in the field, he fell asleep, and he had a dream, and in his dream he heard God say to him. " Go home to your father, and I will be with you."

When Jacob awoke, he sent a servant to fetch Rachel and Leah, for he wanted to speak to them; and he said to them, " God has spoken to me in a dream, and has told me to return home to my father."

Then Rachel and Leah said, " we will go with you."

Then Jacob packed up all his things—his tents and his clothes and his furniture, and all he had. He put his things on the backs of his camels and asses. He placed his wives and his eleven children on camels too. He told his servants to drive all his sheep, cows, goats, and asses and camels. So they all set out.

Laban did not see Jacob go away; for Jacob's tents were not close to the place where Laban lived. At last Laban heard that Jacob was gone: then he was angry, and he went after Jacob, and he begged Jacob to come back; but Jacob would go back to Canaan.

Jacob was pleased to go back to Canaan; but there was one thing that frightened him. He remembered that Esau had once said he would kill him; he was afraid lest he should now come and kill him and his children.

Soon Jacob heard that Esau was coming with four hundred men. Jacob now thought that Esau was coming to kill him. So he began to pray to God, and said, "O God, thou hast been very kind to me, and given me a great many things—do not let Esau come and hurt me, and kill my wives and my little children. Thou didst promise to take care of me." God heard Jacob's prayer.

Jacob thought to himself, "I will send a present to show Esau that I wish to behave kindly to him." So he took a great many goats, and sheep, and cows, and asses, and camels, and told his servants to drive them on before, and to tell Esau that he had sent them as a present. Jacob prayed to God all through that night.

In the morning Jacob looked up and saw Esau coming, and four hundred men with him. Jacob did not run away; but he went up to Esau, and as he walked, he stopped seven times, and bowed down to the ground.

And what was it Esau did?

He ran and put his arms round Jacob's neck and

kissed him, and they both wept. God had made Esau's heart more kind.

How glad Jacob was to find that his brother was grown kind! Jacob had prayed to God to make him kind, and God had heard his prayer.

Esau looked up, and saw Rachel and Leah and the little children; and Esau said, "Who are these?"

And Jacob said, "These are my children, that God has been so kind as to give me."

Then Rachel and Leah bowed themselves to the ground, and the maids bowed themselves, and all the children bowed, even the youngest, who was quite a little child He was Rachel's child, and his name was Joseph.

Then Esau said to Jacob, "I met a great many sheep, and cows, and goats—why did you send them on before you?"

Jacob said, "They were for a present for you."

Esau answered, "I have enough, my brother; keep what you have for yourself."

"Pray take my present," said Jacob, "for God has given me a great deal." And Jacob begged Esau so much to take it that at last he took it.

Esau said to Jacob, "Let us take our journey together: and I will go on first."

But Jacob said, "I cannot go as fast as you do, for I have many little children with me, and young lambs and goats; and if one day we were to drive them too fast, they would die. So Jacob would not go with Esau.

Then Esau went home to his own house, which was a great way off; for Esau did not live in Canaan. But Jacob stayed in the land of Canaan, for he wished to live there.

You see that God had let Jacob come back to Canaan, as he had promised. Jacob did not forget the sweet dream I told you of. He went to that very place once more: he had made a heap of stones to mark the place; so he could find it again. There he built an altar, and offered sacrifices to God, who had been so kind to him. God had given him food and clothes, as he had promised: and he had given him many more things besides; for God had given him wives and children, and servants and cattle; and God had made his brother kind to him, and had let him come back to Canaan. Jacob loved God very much, and thanked him for his kindness.

Has not God been very kind to you, my dear children? Tell me what things he has given. Can you think of ten or twelve things he has given you? Food, clothes, &c. &c. Sometimes people have been unkind to you, and God has made them grow kind. How much you ought to love God!

The Lord who all things did create,
  Doth still his wonders show;
See Esau's heart once filled with hate,
  With sudden love o'erflow.

An humble staff poor Jacob bore,
  When first he left the land;

But now behold his plenteous store,
  And his sweet infant band.

Long since the voice of God he heard.
  Foretelling days of peace;
Now God fulfils his gracious word,
  And bids his troubles cease.

Let every knee before Him bow,
  Who can all wonders do;
All hearts can change, *all gifts* bestow.
  Make *every word* come true.

CHILD.

Sweet promises are made to me
  If I serve God in truth;
Thy wonders great, O let me see,
  Guide of my tender youth;

If any hate or wish me ill,
  Lord fill their hearts with love,
And feed, and clothe, and bless me still;—
  Then waft my soul above.

CHAPTER XI.

JOSEPH, OR THE PIT.

Gen. xxxvii. 1—24.

JACOB saw his old father, Isaac, again; and then Isaac died, and Jacob and Esau buried him in that same cave where Abraham and Sarah had been put: they will rise together at the last day;

for Isaac wished to live in a country that is better than Canaan, that is, in heaven.

Esau, you know did not live in the land of Canaan; but Jacob chose to live in Canaan, with his children and his cattle.

All the sons were grown up to be men, when Benjamin was still a little baby. Joseph was next youngest to Benjamin. He was a big boy, and he was the best of all the children. The ten eldest were wicked men. They used to take care of the sheep and goats; and when Joseph was with them, they grieved him by their wicked behaviour; they were also very unkind to him, and always spoke roughly to him. Jacob loved Joseph the best; and this made the others envious. They hated him, because he was the pet and the darling.

Jacob loved Joseph too much. He gave him a very pretty coat made of many colours, yellow, blue, green, pink, red, purple; and Joseph used to wear it.

It is Satan that makes people envious. We should pray to God to keep us from being envious.

You will hear what wicked things these brothers did, because they were envious of dear, good Joseph.

One night Joseph had a very strange dream. He thought he was in a field of corn with all his brothers, and they were making up large bundles of corn, called sheaves. He thought that each of his brothers made a sheaf, and that all his brothers' sheaves bowed down to his sheaf. Joseph thought this a very strange dream, and he told it to his brothers.

But when they heard it they were very angry, and said, "We suppose you mean that we shall bow down to you, though you are the youngest." And so they hated him more than they had done before.

Soon after Joseph had another strange dream. He thought he saw the sun, moon, and eleven stars *in the sky, and that they* bowed down to him. This dream was more strange than the other; and he told it to his father as well as to his brothers.

His father was surprised, and said, "Does the sun mean me, and the moon your mother, and the stars your brothers, and shall we bow down to you?"

Yet Jacob thought that God had sent the dream to Joseph, and would make it come true; but the brothers were more and more angry.

Now Joseph's brethren had a great many sheep and goats to take care of: and there was not enough of grass for them all, round the tents; so they took their flocks a great way off, that they might eat fresh grass. Joseph staid at home with his old father; and Benjamin staid at home because he was quite a little child.

At last Jacob wished to know how his sons were; so he said to Joseph, "Go and see your brothers, and come back and tell me how they are and how the flocks are."

Joseph was always ready to do what his father wished: so he set out on his way.—He took no ass to ride upon, and no servant; but, putting on his pretty coat, he wished his dear father good-bye. He little thought how long it would be before he should see again that dear father's face.

Joseph went a great way, but could not find his brothers. At last a man saw him, and said, "Whom are you looking for?"

And Joseph answered, "I am looking for my brothers—can you tell me where they are feeding their flocks?"

Then the man told him which way they were gone.

Joseph took a great deal of pains to find his brothers.

Now the brothers saw Joseph coming when he was very far off. They knew that it was Joseph: and they said to each other, "Here this dreamer comes, let us kill him, and throw him into a deep hole, and tell our father that a lion or a bear has eaten him up."

So when Joseph came up to them, they seized hold of him. He came to them full of love and kindness; but they looked fiercely upon him; and he was indeed like a gentle lamb in the midst of lions and tigers. He was like the Lord Jesus when the wicked Jews seized him in the garden.

The brothers were going to kill him, when one

of the brothers, named Reuben, said, "Do not kill him, but only throw him into a pit." This brother was a little kinder than the rest, and meant to take him out of the pit, and bring him back to Jacob. The brothers agreed not to kill him. But first they took off his pretty coat.

O how bitterly he cried when he saw what they were going to do to him! how he begged them to spare him, and to let him return to his father!—but they would not hear;* for their hearts were harder than stone.

They threw him into the deep, dark pit; and there he lay hungry and thirsty and weary—without one drop of water to quench his thirst. How it must have grieved Joseph to think that he should not return to his dear father; and his father perhaps would think that he was dead!

The wicked brothers cared not for his groans, but they sat down and began to eat their dinner.

God saw them from his throne in heaven, and was much displeased.

* We are verily guilty concerning our brother, in that we saw the anguish of his soul, when he besought us, and we would not hear. —Gen. xlii. 21.

CHAPTER XII.

JOSEPH, OR THE SLAVE.

Gen. xxxvii. 24—35.

While the brothers were eating their dinner, they looked up and saw some people coming along. As the people came nearer, they saw camels and men riding on them. I will tell you who these men were.

They lived in a country a great way off, and had been to some hills where very sweet things grew, called spice and balm. They had plucked these sweet things and had put them in large bundles on the backs of their camels. They were going to carry them to a country a great way off, and to sell them for money.

This was their way of getting their living, and it was a good way; yet they were wicked men, as you will see.

One of the brothers, called Judah, said, "Let us sell Joseph to those men; for it would be better to sell him than to kill him: we shall get some money if we sell him; and it would be very cruel to kill Joseph, as he is our brother."

Yet was it not very cruel to sell Joseph? This brother was not really kind. The other brothers said that they thought it was a good plan to sell Joseph. So they called to the men, and asked them if they would buy a young boy.

And the men said, "Yes." This was wicked.

"How much will you give us for him?" said the brothers.

"We will give you twenty pieces of silver," said the men.

Then Joseph's brothers pulled Joseph out of the pit. Perhaps he thought that they were going to let him return to his father.

Ah! poor Joseph! He soon found that his brothers were not going to be kind. The men and the camels were waiting outside the pit. The men paid the money to the brothers, and then took Joseph and carried him away with them.

When Joseph was gone, the brothers said, "What shall we tell our father when he asks us where Joseph is?—we will not say we have seen Joseph, but we will say we have found his coat on the ground."

Then the brothers killed one of their young goats, and dipped the pretty coat in the blood. "We will show our father this bloody coat," said they. So they carried the coat home, all covered with blood, and the money for which they had sold Joseph.

Do you think they were happy in their hearts? O no! The wicked cannot be happy. God had written down their wickedness in his book.

Poor Joseph with the wicked men was not so unhappy as they: for God was his friend. Old Jacob had been thinking of his sons while they were gone. How glad he must have been when he heard the bleating of their sheep, and knew they were come home! He must have looked to see whether Joseph was with them. But no. His sons came up to him. In their hands they held a bloody coat. They showed it to Jacob, and said, "We have found this—Do you think it is your son's coat or not?"

Jacob knew that coat, and said, "It is my son's coat; a lion or bear has eaten him up, and has torn Joseph to pieces."

How Jacob wept for his darling child! How sorry he was that he had sent him alone to seek his brothers! The wicked brothers tried to comfort Jacob, and said, "Do not weep so much," but Jacob would not hear.

"No; I shall die; and then I shall be with Joseph, for I shall never be happy any more."

How sad it was for this old man, leaning on his stick, his hair grey, and his face full of sadness, while he thought that his dear boy was eaten up by the lion or the bear! His little Benjamin was a comfort to him. Jacob would never let him go away, nor would he trust him with his brothers, though he did not know how wicked they had been.

These brothers first had envied Joseph, then they had told a lie to hide their sin.

Children sometimes try to hide their faults by telling lies, and so they make God more angry than he was before. My dear children, remember that God always sees you; and that he hates liars, and will not let them live with him in glory.

What anguish once poor Joseph felt,
When he before his brethren knelt,
And loud for mercy cried!*
Refusing still to hear his pray'r,
In blood they dipp'd his garment fair,
And sought their guilt to hide.

Now by the heathen-stranger band,
Away from his dear native land,
The weeping youth is borne:
His father shall feel bitter pangs,
When he shall hear some lion's fangs
Those tender lambs have torn.

A precious load the camels bear
Of balm, and myrrh, and spices rare,
Which scatter sweetness round:
But sweeter than the sweetest spice,
True piety beyond all price
In Joseph's heart is found.

Blessings shall rest upon his head
Where'er his wandering steps are led,
For he to God is dear;
And this same God shall with him go,
With heav'nly comforts soothe his wo,
And chase away his fear.

* We saw the anguish of his soul, when he besought us, and we would not hear.—Gen. xlii. 21.

CHAPTER XIII.

JOSEPH, OR THE PRISONER.

Gen. xxxix.

THE men who had bought Joseph, took him to a country a great way off. It was called Egypt.

When they got to Egypt they tried to sell him, as if he had been a horse or a cow. In some countries men are sold, and are called slaves. Poor Joseph was sold as a slave. Do you not hope that a kind man bought him? And it was a kind man that bought him. There was a very rich man who knew the king, and he bought Joseph to be his slave. His name was Potiphar. He took Joseph home with him. He did not send him to work in the field; but he made him a servant in the house. So Joseph had not very hard work to do.

Joseph tried to be a good servant. Though he wished very much to be with his father, he did not waste his time in fretting, but took great pains to please his master. When his master told him to do anything, he did it so well that his master was quite pleased with him. It was God that made Joseph able to do his work so well; and Joseph's master knew that it was God that helped him to do things well.* I suppose that Joseph had told him; for his master did not know the true God, but worshipped idols.

His master liked him better every day. At last, his master said to Joseph, "I can trust you so well that I will give you the charge of the other servants when I am out. Take care of the house, and all the things in it, of the garden and of the fields; for I can trust you."

So Joseph had the care of everything, and all the other servants minded what he said: and he might do what he liked when his master was out. But Joseph behaved the same as if his master were watching him; for he knew the eye of God was always upon him. There are many children who behave ill as soon as their parents go out of the room: such children do not fear God.

Though Joseph had the care of nice things to eat, and beautiful things to wear, he only took what his master allowed him to take. He was always busy—sometimes in the house, and sometimes in the field: and God made the things grow well in the field, and the work to go on right in the house.

So that Potiphar had no trouble himself, but found that Joseph would manage all for him.

So Joseph had now all he could wish for; but he could not forget his father, and his little baby

* And his master *saw* that the Lord was with him, and that the Lord *made* all that he did to prosper in his hand.—Gen. xxxix. 3.

brother Benjamin. As for his mother, Rachel, you know that she had died some time before.

Now you shall hear what a sad thing happened to Joseph.

Potiphar had a very wicked wife. She wished Joseph to be turned out of the house: for Joseph had found out how bad she was; so she did not like to see Joseph.

This wicked woman said to Potiphar, "Your slave, Joseph, that you think so good, is very wicked, and when you are out he behaves very ill." Then she told Potiphar of bad things that she said Joseph had done.

Potiphar was so foolish as to believe her, and he fell into a great rage, and said, "Joseph shall be put into prison."

So some men took Joseph, and brought him to the prison, which was in Potiphar's house.

Were you ever in a prison, my dear child? It is a dark place, with very little windows, and bars of iron before the windows, and iron gates and bolts.

Joseph was put in prison; and his feet were hurt by great iron chains, which were fastened round them.*

There were a great many men in the prison, and most of them had done very bad things, but Joseph had done nothing wrong. God still loved

* Joseph was sold for a servant, whose feet they hurt with fetters Ps. cv. 17, 18.

Joseph, and he could make him happy even in a prison.

There was a man who kept the keys of the prison, and took care of the prisoners; he was called the keeper of the prison. Sometimes keepers are very unkind; but God put it into the keeper's heart to love Joseph. Joseph had a very sweet countenance or look, and he behaved well to the keeper, and minded all he said.

At last, the keeper took the chains off Joseph's feet, and allowed him to walk about the prison, and take care of the prisoners. The keeper found that he could trust him, and that Joseph managed things well. It was God who made Joseph do everything so well; for God was Joseph's friend, and was always watching over him to comfort him.

Joseph hoped that God would some day let him get out of prison.

See Joseph in a prison cast,
In darkness under ground
His feet within the stocks made fast,
With iron fetters bound;
Can this be he (now clad in raiment vile)
Who lately shar'd a father's tend'rest smile?

But in the prison shines a light,
Which none but Joseph sees;
The promises of God are bright,
And give his spirit ease;
The day shall come, when he with honour crown'd
Shall see his brethren bending low around.

Yes, God shall clear his innocence,
And make it fully known,

Yes, God shall send and draw him thence,
And raise him to a throne;
But first, like gold, his patience must be tried,
And (as by fire) his heart be purified.*

CHAPTER XIV.

JOSEPH, OR THE BUTLER AND BAKER.

Gen. xl.

THE prison, you remember, was in the house of Potiphar. One day, Potiphar brought two men to Joseph, and said to Joseph, "Take great care that these men do not get out of prison. I give them under your charge." So you see Potiphar thought Joseph could be trusted: perhaps he had found out that Joseph was not so bad as he had once thought; still he did not let Joseph out of prison.

I will tell you who these men were that Potiphar brought to Joseph. They were the servants of the king of Egypt. The king of Egypt had a great many servants to wait on him. One of his servants used to bring him wine in a cup to drink. This servant was called his butler. Another man used to bake things for his dinner, and bring them to the king. He was called the baker.

The butler and the baker had both offended the

* That the trial of your faith, being much more precious than of gold that perisheth, though it be tried with fire, might be found unto praise, and honour, and glory, &c.—1 Peter, i. 7.

king: I do not know what they had done, but they had made the king so angry that he had said they should be shut up in prison.

So the king had said to Potiphar, the great captain, "Put these men in the prison."

Then Potiphar brought them to Joseph, and told him to keep them safe. Joseph shut them up in a room together, and gave them bread and water every day, and took great care of them.

One morning when Joseph came to see them, he observed that they looked very sad indeed. So Joseph said to them, "Why do you look so very sad?"

Then they answered, "We have each had a very strange dream to-night, and we think our dreams have some meaning, but we cannot find it out and there is nobody in the prison who can tell us."

Then Joseph said, "But my God knows all things: he could tell me the meaning. Only tell me your dreams."

The butler told his dream the first. He said, "I thought I saw a tree such as grapes grow upon —*a vine.* It had three branches, but no grapes. While I was looking, I saw little buds, and they turned into grapes, and they grew ripe. I picked the grapes, and squeezed them into a cup, and made wine, and then brought the cup to the king for him to drink, as I used to do."

This was the butler's dream, and God told Joseph the meaning of it.

"You saw three branches," said Joseph;

"something will happen to you in three days. The king will send for you to be his butler again."

When the baker heard this pleasant meaning, he thought that his dream would be pleasant too: so he began to tell it. The baker said, "I dreamt that I was carrying three white baskets on my head, the one on the top of the other. In the baskets there were baked meats, and birds came and picked the meat out of the top basket."

The baker thought that Joseph would say, "In three days you shall be baker again to the king." But this dream had a sad meaning.

"Something will happen to you in three days," said Joseph. "The king will send for you, and will hang you upon a tree, and the birds will pick your flesh off your bones."

So while the butler was pleased with what Joseph had told him, the poor baker was very sorry, because he knew that he must die.

Joseph had one little favour to ask of the butler. You can guess what it was. "When you are with the king of Egypt," said Joseph, "giving him his wine, will you tell him about me? Tell him how I am shut up in prison, and cannot get out. I once lived in a land a great way off, and I was stolen away, and now I am shut up in this prison, though I have done nothing wicked to deserve it. Beg the king to let me out."

You see Joseph did not tell of his brothers' wickedness in having sold him.

In three days the king sent some men to the

prison to fetch the butler and the baker. It was the king's birth-day, and he had made a feast for his servants, and he had thought of the butler and baker, and had said, "Let the butler come back to me, and let the baker be hanged; I will not forgive him." So now both the butler and the baker knew that Joseph had told them the truth.

Did the butler remember Joseph when he was with the king? No, he forgot him. I suppose he was thinking of the fine things he saw, of eating and drinking, of money and clothes, and forgot that poor Joseph was in a prison. The butler was unkind, and worse than unkind; he was ungrateful. Joseph had been kind to him, yet he was not kind in return; therefore I call him ungrateful. Many children are ungrateful to their parents, who were kind to them when they were little; and all people are ungrateful to God, who has given his Son to die for them.

Poor Joseph waited in vain. No one came to let him out of prison. One day passed, and then another: summer came, and then winter, but Joseph was still shut up. Yet God had not forgotten him. Why did God make him wait so long? That he might learn to be patient. My dear child, if God lets you be sick a long while, it is to make you patient. You should think to yourself, "God will make me well when he thinks best: but perhaps he means to take me to heaven instead."

And has the butler, then, forgot
Poor Joseph's last request;

Nor of the tender pity thought,
  Shown to him when distrest ?

Why does he not of Joseph speak,
  When he the cup presents,
Implore the king his bonds to break,
  And show his innocence ?

Content, within the palace gay,
  He lives on princely fare ;
While Joseph mourns the light of day,
  And breathes the prison air.

But while the butler I accuse
  Of hateful selfishness,
O let me not in pride refuse
  My own sins to confess.

Have I remembered all the good
  My parents have bestowed,
And in their woes done all I could
  To ease their heavy load ?

And have I not ungrateful been
  Unto the God of love,
And often griev'd him by my sin,
  And with his Spirit strove ?*

Yet Jesus, since he left the grave,
  To sit upon his throne,
Still intercedes with God to save
  Us, who in prison groan.†

Grieve not the Holy Spirit of God.—Eph. iv. 30

† He is able also to save them to the uttermost, that come unto God by him; seeing he ever liveth to make intercession for them.—Heb vii. 25.

CHAPTER XV.

JOSEPH, OR THE RELEASE.

I HAVE told you of the great king of Egypt. He was the king of the country where Joseph was. His name was Pharaoh. He had a great many servants, as I told you. He sat upon a throne, wore beautiful clothes, a chain of gold round his neck, a ring upon his hand, and a crown of gold upon his head. He lived in a fine house, and rode out in a chariot drawn by many horses; and as he passed by, people bowed down to the ground. One night, this great king had two very strange dreams. I will tell you what they were.

He thought he was standing by a river, and that seven fat cows came out of the river, and began to eat the grass that grew near. This was a pleasant sight; but, soon after, he saw seven very thin cows, (more ugly than any cows he had ever seen.) come out of the river; and they ate up the seven fat cows; and yet, after they had eaten them, they looked as thin as they did before. Then the king awoke.

But soon he fell asleep, and dreamt that he saw a stalk of corn with seven fine ears growing on it. While he was looking, he saw another stalk with seven very bad ears of corn on it; and these bad ears ate up the seven good ears.

These were Pharaoh's two dreams. He thought

them very strange, and longed to know the meaning of them. In the morning he told his servants to find some people who said they could tell the meaning of dreams. A great many men came who pretended to be wise; but they could not tell the king the meaning of his dreams. The king was very unhappy, but what could he do?

At last the butler thought of Joseph. He had not thought of him for a long while, and now he felt sorry. He said to the king, "I do remember my faults this day. You know, O king, that you were once angry with me and with your baker, and you shut us up in prison, in the house of the captain Potiphar. While we were in prison, the baker and I each had a dream, and a young man, a servant, told us the meaning of our dreams, and said that the baker would be hanged, and that I should be let out of prison; and so it was, the baker was hanged, and you sent for me back to be your butler, just as the young man had said." Then Pharaoh told his servants to fetch this young man out of prison.

So the servants came to the prison, and said to the keeper, "We are come to fetch Joseph; the king wants to speak to him."

Joseph must have been glad to hear this. He saw that God had heard his prayer. Joseph was dressed in very poor clothes, not fit for a king to see. So the servants gave him neat clothes, and brought him to the king.

It was a long, long while, since Joseph had felt

the sweet air blow upon his face, and since he had seen the green fields. I think he must have look ed pale and sick.

He came into the king's fine house, and stood before him. The king said, " I hear that you can tell the meaning of dreams."

" It is not I myself," said Joseph, "that can tell the meaning, but my God can, and I know that he will tell the meaning of your dreams." Then Pharaoh told Joseph his two dreams—the dream about the seven cows, and the dream about the seven ears.

When he had done speaking, Joseph answered, " Both your dreams have the same meaning. This is what is going to happen. The next seven years a great deal of corn will grow in the fields; but afterwards hardly any corn will grow in the fields for seven years. The seven fat cows meant the seven years, when much corn would grow; and the seven thin cows meant the seven years when very little corn would grow. God sent you these dreams, that you might know what is going to happen."

Now what could the king do? First there would be a great deal of corn, then scarcely any. Could you, my little child, advise the king what to do? Joseph gave him some advice. He said, " Save up some of the corn, when there is so much, that you may have some, when there is none growing in the fields. You should look for a very wise man, who will save up the corn, and put it in large barns; or the people will die when no corn grows in the fields."

Pharaoh was much pleased with Joseph for telling him the meaning of his dreams; he believed what Joseph said, and so did all Pharaoh's servants. And the king Pharaoh said to his servants, "Where can I find so wise a man as Joseph? He shall save up the corn."

Then Pharaoh said to Joseph, "You are so very wise that you shall help me to manage all the people in the land. Every one shall mind you as they do me, and you shall be the greatest person next to me."

Then Pharaoh took the ring off his hand, and put it on Joseph's hand; and he gave him beautiful clothes like his own, and a gold chain to wear round his neck. He gave him a fine chariot to ride in, and desired people to bow down when they saw him.

So Joseph was made a great Lord; but he would not be idle. He went about all the country in his chariot to get corn, and he built large barns everywhere, and filled them with corn, and so he did for seven years. He did not spend his time eating and drinking, but was always doing good to people.

He was very glad he was let out of prison, and he thanked God very much. He was not happy because he wore fine clothes: but he was glad to be able to do good to people, by saving up corn. He married a wife, and he had two little boys; yet still he thought of his dear old father, and hoped that he should one day see him again; and he thought of little Benjamin, and hoped his brothers had not killed him, nor put him in a pit, and he hoped that his brothers were sorry for their wickedness. He did not feel angry with his brothers. Joseph knew that it was God who had let them sell him for a slave, and that God had let them do it that he might save up corn in Egypt.

It is God that makes all things happen;* and God has wise reasons for all he does. If he lets us be sick, it is for some good reason. One day we shall know why God let us be sick, or let wicked people hurt us, or take away our things.†

You know why God let wicked people kill the Lord Jesus. It was that he might die instead of us, and save us from hell.

Behold him in a chariot riding,
  Who lately in a prison lay;
The king, to him all pow'r confiding,
  Deck'd him with gold and white array.

Now hear the servants loud proclaiming,
  "Bow low the knee before his car!"
While ev'ry mouth is Joseph naming—
  "My Lord Zaph-nath paaneah."

Through all the land he goes exploring,
  Gath'ring the precious fruits of earth;

* Shall there be evil in a city, and the Lord hath not done it?—Amos iii. 6.

† What I do thou knowest not now; but thou shalt know here after—John xiii 7.

In spacious barns the harvest storing,
  Against the dreadful days of dearth.

How well is Joseph's faith rewarded,
  Which made him long in patience wait;
God has at length relief afforded,
  And rais'd him to his glorious state.

And God will every soul deliver
  That puts his trust in him alone;
And wipe away his tears for ever,
  And raise him to a heav'nly throne!

CHAPTER XVI.

JOSEPH, OR THE LORD OF EGYPT.

Gen. xlii.

You have heard, my dear children, how Joseph was made almost as great as the king. A great deal of corn grew in the fields next year and the year after, and for seven years after the king's dream. But then scarcely any corn grew. The poor people came to king Pharaoh, and said, "We have nothing to eat, and we shall die." Then Pharaoh said, "Go to Joseph; he can help you." So the people went to Joseph and he opened his large barns full of corn, and sold the corn to the people. They brought money, and large bags or sacks. Joseph took the money and filled the sacks with corn. A great many people came to buy corn. Some from a long way off; but Joseph had enough corn for all.

Among the people who came there were ten men who had come from a far country. Each of them had an ass, and on the ass a sack, and in their hands they brought money. Who do you think these were? They were Joseph's brothers. When Joseph saw them he remembered them, though he had not seen them for twenty years. He knew those cruel brothers, who had sold him for twenty pieces of silver. If he pleased he might have punished them. He might have told his servants to kill them. Do you think Joseph will punish his brothers, or do you think he will be kind to them? Now you shall hear how he behaved to them.

The brothers thought Joseph was a great lord, and they did not know that they had seen him before; for he wore fine clothes, and he was grown to be a man, and he had another name, which the king had given him.

So when the ten brothers saw him they bowed upon the ground before him. Then Joseph remembered his dream about the sheaves bowing down to his sheaf, and he saw that God had made it come true.

Joseph felt ready to forgive his brothers; but he wished first to see whether they where sorry for their wickedness, and whether they loved their father and little Benjamin; Joseph did not tell them who he was. He even pretended to be unkind. He spoke to them in a rough voice, and said, "Where do you come from?"

"From the land of Canaan," they said, "to buy food."

But Joseph said he did not believe they spoke truth. "You come," he said, "to see what a bad land this is, with no corn growing in it, and you mean to bring some king with soldiers to fight us."

"No, indeed," said Joseph's brothers, "we do not. We are ten poor brothers and we are come to buy food."

But Joseph said he would not believe what they said.

Joseph's brothers answered, "We are all brothers, and once there were twelve of us, but one is dead, and the youngest is with our father, who is an old man." They tried to make Joseph believe what they said, but he would not; that is, he pretended not to believe them.

At last Joseph said, "I must see your youngest brother. I shall send one of you to fetch him, and I shall keep the rest in prison, till he comes back with the youngest brother."

The brothers were much frightened when they heard this; for they knew their father would not choose to part with Benjamin, lest he should be killed. So not one of the brothers said he would go and fetch Benjamin.

Joseph put them all in prison, and kept them shut up together for three days. While they were shut up, they had time to think of their wickedness to Joseph.

When people are shut up they have time to think and to pray. I hope, dear children, when you are shut up, as a punishment, that you pray to God to make you good. The brothers were very much frightened; they did not know what Joseph was going to do with them.

At last Joseph came to them in the prison, and said, "This is what you must do, and then you shall live; for I fear God."

How glad and surprised the brothers must have been when they heard him say he feared God! for the other people worshipped idols.

Joseph said, "I will only keep one of you shut up in the prison, all the rest of you may go back, and take corn home with you; but when you come again, you must bring your youngest brother with you; or I shall think you have not spoken truth; but, if you do bring him, I will believe you."

The brothers were glad to think they might go back, yet it made them sad to hear that one of them would be kept in prison. They remembered their wickedness to Joseph, and they said one to another, "It was very wicked in us to treat him as we did. How he begged us to spare him, and we would not; and now God is punishing us for it."

Joseph heard what they said, and it made the tears run down his cheeks; so that he was obliged to go out of the room to weep. He did not like to see them unhappy; but you know he wanted to find out whether they were kind to Benjamin, and whether they loved their old father, and whether they were sorry for all they had done.

When Joseph came back, he took one of the brothers, called Simeon, and said that he would keep him in prison till the others brought their youngest brother with them. So Joseph had Simeon bound with ropes, or chains, while the other brothers stood round.

Then they must have remembered how once poor Joseph had been bound, and sold for a slave.

Simeon was left alone in the prison, and he did not know whether his brothers would ever come back, and whether he would ever be let out.

Before the brothers set off to go home, Joseph said to his servants, " When you fill those men's sacks with corn, put back into their sacks the money that they paid me for it, and give them also some food by the way." Joseph wished his poor brothers to have something to eat by the way. And the servant did as Joseph told him; but Joseph's brethren did not know what the servant had done.

How glad these brothers where to get away from Egypt, and to come back to their father, and to their little children, who had scarcely anything left to eat!

When they were come home, they told their father all that had happened. " There was a great lord," they said, " who sold corn to the people; and he spoke very roughly to us, and said that we were not come to buy corn, but that we only wanted to see the land, that we might bring men to fight the poor hungry people that lived there. He called us 'spies.' We told him that we were not spies, but were twelve brothers;—that one was dead, and that one was with our father in the land of Canaan. But that lord would not believe us, and told us we must bring our youngest brother with us; and he took Simeon, and shut him up in prison, and said that he would not let him out till we came back with Benjamin."

Poor old Jacob was very sad when he heard all this. Then the brothers began to open their sacks of corn, and they were quite surprised to find their money at the top of their sacks; but they were not pleased; they thought that some one had put the money there to get them in disgrace, and that when they went back to Egypt, they should be punished for stealing; so they were very much frightened.

They had not stolen this money; but they were thieves, for they once had stolen Joseph, and sold him for twenty pieces of silver. God knew that they were thieves.

They were more afraid than ever of going back to Egypt, and seeing the great lord; yet they wished very much to go, for they had only bought a little corn, and they wanted more: and they knew that poor Simeon would remain in prison till they went back to Egypt.

How could they persuade Jacob to let Benjamin go? For Jacob said, "No, I cannot trust Benjamin with you, lest some harm should happen to him. You have taken away two of my children, Joseph and Simeon, and you would not bring Benjamin back if I were to let him go. If any evil were to happen to him, you would bring down my gray hairs with sorrow to the grave." Jacob felt that it would break his heart to lose Benjamin, he loved him so very much.

So the brothers were obliged to stay in Canaan; for they knew it would be of no use to go to Egypt, except Benjamin went with them. What trouble they now were in! God was punishing them for their wickedness.

Famine had spread on ev'ry side,
  And thousands flock'd from distant lands
To Joseph, who their need supplied
  From stores as countless as the sands.

Amongst the rest a troop appear'd,—
  Full well were they to Joseph known;
Their cruel looks he once had fear'd,
  When in the pit they cast him down.

Those features he could recollect,
  Though worn by care, and scorch'd by heat;
But little did those men suspect
  They bent around their brother's seat.

The youthful bloom had left his cheek;
  Grave and majestic was his air;
A language strange they heard him speak,
  And splendid garments saw him wear.

He spoke to them in tone severe,
  And made them all their hist'ry tell,

And glad was he no tale to hear
  Of wo and death that had befel.

Yet Joseph would his name conceal,
  Nor his own tender love express;
Until he saw his brothers feel
  Sorrow for their past wickedness.

But while he caus'd them grief and pain,
  Compassion fill'd his gentle heart;
His tears he could not long restrain,
  But stepp'd aside, and wept apart.

CHILD.

Thus my dear Saviour felt for me,
  Before I lov'd him as my friend;—
Did then each tear with pity see,
  To ev'ry sigh and groan attend.*

CHAPTER XVII.

JOSEPH, OR THE FEAST.

Gen. xliii.

As the brothers could not persuade old Jacob to let Benjamin go with them, they were obliged to stay in Canaan. Soon they had eaten up all their corn, and none grew in their fields, and what could they do for food?

* It is said of rebellious Israel, "In all their affliction he was afflicted."—Isa. lxiii. 9.
God also says to Israel, "I have loved thee with an *everlasting* love.'—Jer. xxxi. 3.

Jacob saw how hungry they were, and at last he said, "Go again, buy us a little food."

Then they said, "We cannot go without Benjamin, for the man who sold corn said we should not see him, unless we brought our youngest brother. If you will let Benjamin come with us, then we will go."

Jacob was very unhappy when he heard this, and he said, "Why did you tell the man you had a brother? it was behaving very unkindly to me to tell him."

Then the brothers answered, "The man asked us so many questions. He said to us, "Is your father alive? Have you another brother? Could we think that he would say, "Bring your youngest brother?"

Still Jacob did not like to let Benjamin go.

One of the brothers (called Judah) said, "I will take care of Benjamin, if you will let him go. I promise to bring him back to you; and if I do not, I will take all the blame. For we and our little children shall die, if you do not let him come."

Jacob saw it was of no use to refuse any more, or they would all die, and Benjamin too. So he gave Benjamin into the care of Judah.

But Jacob was afraid of the man being unkind to them, and of his saying they had stolen the money. So he said to them, "Bring the man a present."

What could they bring? They had gardens with fruit and flowers growing in them.

"Pick some nuts and almonds off your trees," said Jacob, "and take a little of that sweet stuff called balm and myrrh; and take some spices, and a little honey, and take them with you as a present to the man."

The man was very rich, and did not want anything, but the present would show that they wished to please him.

"Besides," said Jacob, "take the money back that you found in your sacks—take more money in your hands to buy more corn, and take Benjamin, and go to the man."

Jacob's heart was full of pain when he said this.

Then he began to pray to God. "May God give you mercy before the man, and send home Simeon and Benjamin."

This was Jacob's prayer.

"Now," said he, "if I must lose my children, I must lose them."

When Jacob wished his dear Benjamin good-bye, he thought of how he once had parted with his Joseph, the day he sent him to look for his brothers, when he put on his pretty coat, but never returned.

Now Jacob feared that he should never see Benjamin again.

The brothers took the present, the sweet present, with them, and they each took some money in their hands, and they took their asses, and their empty sacks; and Judah took care of Benjamin.

So they parted from their old father, and their wives, and their little children, and they set out on their journey.

They all felt very sad that day. The brothers were frightened. They were afraid they should be taken up as thieves when they got to Egypt.

At last they came to Egypt. They went to the place where Joseph was selling the corn, and he saw them. He looked to see whether Benjamin was with them. How pleased he was to see him!

Benjamin was a baby when Joseph had seen him last, yet Joseph knew that it was Benjamin.

As soon as he saw his brothers, he called his chief servant, who managed his house, and said to him. "Take those ten men to my house, and get a great dinner ready, for they must dine with me to day."

The brothers did not hear what Joseph said to the servant. The servant came to them, and told them to come with him. So they came, and he brought them to Joseph's own house—a fine large house. Yet the brothers were not pleased, but very much frightened.

"Ah!" said they to each other, "we are going to be put in prison: and we shall be kept in Egypt, to work hard, we and our asses."

They thought of their poor father, and of what he would do.

When they got to the door of the house, they

came up to the servant, and said, "O sir, we came here once before to buy a little food, and we paid money for it; but when we got home we opened our sacks, and found the money in them, and here we have brought it back; and we have brought more money to buy more corn. We cannot tell who put the money in our sacks."

It *was* quite right in the brothers to bring back the money; but once they had stolen money. Now they were speaking truth, but once they had told lies.

The servant answered them very kindly, and said, "Fear not, God is your Father—God gave you that money, and put the money in your sacks."

You see the servant knew about God. Who could have taught him about God? The people in Egypt worshipped idols. It must have been Joseph who had taught his servant.

How happy the brothers were now! They soon found that they were not going to be put into a prison, but that they were to dine in a fine house. What could make the man grow so kind? They did not know the reason.

While they were waiting, the servant went and brought poor Simeon out of prison. He had been shut up a long while. I hope when he was in prison, that he had thought of his having once put Joseph in the pit.

The servant told them that dinner would not be ready till twelve o'clock: and while they were waiting, he brought them water to wash their feet, and he gave some food to their poor, tired, and hungry asses.

The brothers said, "Let us get our present ready, while we are waiting for the lord to come in."

So they went out, and got ready the balm and spices, the honey, and nuts, and almonds.

At last Joseph came in from selling the corn, and the brothers came into the house, and brought the present in their hand, and they bowed down upon the ground. The eleven brothers bowed down, as the eleven sheaves had done in the dream.

This time Joseph spoke very kindly to them. He asked them how they were; but most of all he wanted to know how his dear father was.

"Is your father well?" he asked. "You said you had an old father. Is he yet alive?"

They said, "Yes, our father is well, and he is alive;" and as they spoke, they bowed down their heads to the ground.

Then Joseph looked for Benjamin, and when he saw him, he longed to throw his arms round his neck, and kiss him, but he would not do it yet. He only said, "Is this your younger brother that you told me of?"

And then he made this little prayer, "God be gracious to thee, my son."

When Joseph had said this, he felt the tears coming into his eyes, and he could not help crying; so he went quickly out of the room, and shut himself up in his own room, and there he cried by himself. He was a very tender-hearted man, and he loved this young brother very much.

One reason why he loved him was, that Benjamin was the son of his own mother, Rachel, while all the others had another mother, Leah; for Jacob, you know, had two wives.

Now the dinner was ready; so Joseph would not stay in his room; but first he washed his face, that no one might see that he had been crying, and then he tried to look cheerful, and he said to his servants, "Put the dinner on the table."

In the room where they were to dine, there were three tables. One was for Joseph's servants, another was for Joseph himself, (for he always dined at a table by himself,) and the other table was for the eleven brothers.

Joseph told them where to sit: he made the eldest sit first, and then the second, just according to their age, and he made Benjamin sit last. The brothers were surprised at Joseph's knowing which was eldest and which was second, for it is hard to tell how old a grown up man is; but Joseph knew them better than they thought he did.

Now they all sat down to dinner. It was long since they had eaten such a dinner, and they had made a great journey, and were tired, and hungry, and thirsty. Joseph sent them nice things from his table; but he sent five times as much to Benjamin as to any of the others.

Were the brothers envious of Benjamin, because

Joseph sent him the most? No, they were not. Once they had been envious of Joseph—but now they were not envious. They ate and drank, and they were merry.

Joseph could see them all—and it was a pleasant sight to him. Once they had eaten their dinner, while he lay in the pit, and they had given him none. Yet he would not treat them so, but would return good for evil.

You remember how kindly Jesus behaved to people who were unkind to him. God is kind to us though we do many things to offend him. If a child is unkind to you, should you be unkind too? If your brother has a cake, and will not give you any—if you afterwards have a cake, should you give him some, or should you not? Oh! you should do as Joseph did, and be kind to those who have been unkind to you.

Ah! what has caused this sudden change
In him, who lately seem'd so strange,
And on his brothers frown'd?
And now their very beasts are fed,
For them a princely table's spread,
With sumptuous dainties crown'd.

Young Benjamin is with them now,
And Joseph has unbent his brow,
And on his brothers smil'd:
For much he hopes that envious rage
No more those brother's hearts engage
Against a favourite child.

What tenderness fills Joseph's breast!
He sees the babe* whom he caress'd,
His own dear mother's son:
His lips with blessings overflow,
And larger messes help to show
Which is the favour'd one.

But while he this distinction makes,
No hateful jealousy awakes,
But all the gladness share.
A little more will Joseph prove
The strength and fervour of his love,
And then his own declare.

CHILD.

Can I another bear to see
Preferr'd and honour'd above me,
And feel no inward pain?
Then in my heart will Jesus dwell,
For these kind feelings please him well,
And shall his love obtain.†

But no such flowers by nature grow
Within the human heart below,
Since Adam's shameful fall.‡
Then, if I would my Saviour please,
I must, upon my bended knees,
For his sweet Spirit call.§

* When Joseph was sold into Egypt, it is supposed that Benjamin was still an infant.

† Jesus answered and said unto him, "If any man love me he will keep my words: and my Father will love him, and we wil. come unto him, and make our abode with him."—John xiv. 23.

Live in peace; and the God of love and peace shall be with you." -2 Cor. xiii. 11.

‡ In me (that is, in my flesh) dwelleth no good thing.—Rom vii. 16.

§ The fruit of the Spirit is love.—Gal. v. 22.

CHAPTER XVIII

JOSEPH, OR THE FORGIVING BROTHER.

Gen. xliv.; xlv. 1—15.

The brothers spent a happy day with Joseph. They did not go home that day, but waited to set out on the morrow.

You know that they had come to buy corn, and they had brought empty sacks with them. Joseph called his servant, and said to him secretly, "Fill the sacks of those eleven men with corn, and put their money that they have given me for the corn back into their sacks. And put my silver cup into the sack of the youngest."

The servant filled the sacks with corn, and put the money into them. And he put the silver cup into Benjamin's sack: and then he gave the sacks to the brothers. They did not know that the servant had put money or a cup into them.

The next morning, as soon as it was light, the brothers rose up, took their asses and their sacks, and set off, to return home to their father. How glad they were to get away safely—not one left behind!

What a pleasant history they thought they should have to tell their father! How much surprised he would be to hear of the great lord's kindness, and how glad he would be to see Benjamin again!

But soon was all their joy turned into grief.

They *had* gone but a little way, when some one called them. It was Joseph's servant; he came running after them.

"What has made you," said he, "behave so ill to my lord, after all his kindness to you? Why have you stolen his silver cup, out of which he drinks?"

The brothers were much surprised to hear that the cup was stolen.

"Why should you think," said they, "that we have taken it? we would not do such a wicked thing. Did we not bring back the money, when we thought it had been put in our sacks by mistake? And now would we steal a silver cup out of your lord's house? None of us have taken it. If one of us have taken it, let him die, and let all the rest be slaves to your lord."

They said this, because they were quite sure that none of them had taken it.

"No," said the servant, "it shall not be so; the one who has taken the cup shall not be killed; he shall only be a slave to my lord, and the others shall not be slaves; they shall all go home."

Then the servants told them to open their sacks; so the eldest brother took down his sack; the servant looked in among the corn, but could find no cup. Then the second opened his sack, but there was no cup hid in it. The third showed his, and each brother showed his in his turn. At last Benjamin showed his. How much were they all surprised when they found the silver cup in it!

You know that Benjamin had not stolen it. You know that the servant had put it in the sack when he filled it with corn.

The servant said to Benjamin, "You must come back with me to my lord." He was going to take him for a slave, and never let him return home; but he said that his brothers might go home.

And would they go and leave Benjamin behind?

"No," said they, "we will go back with Benjamin."

You see that they loved Benjamin, and they would not leave him alone in his distress.

They put their sacks again on their asses, and followed the servant to Joseph's house. Their hearts were bursting with grief, and they cried as they went.

Joseph was in his house, waiting for them.

Joseph was very glad to see them all come back with Benjamin, and to see them crying so much lest Benjamin should be kept to be a slave. Now Joseph saw that they loved Benjamin very much.

When they saw Joseph, they fell on their faces on the ground.

Joseph spoke to them as if he was angry, and said, "What is this wicked thing that you have done?"

Do you remember that Judah had promised to take care of Benjamin? So Judah began to beg Joseph to forgive Benjamin.

Judah knew that it would be of no use to say that Benjamin had not taken the cup, so he only begged Joseph to take pity on them.

"God is punishing us for our sins," said Judah, "and we can say nothing: we must all be your slaves.

"No," said Joseph, "not all, only he who stole the cup; he shall be my slave; let the others go back to their father."

Joseph wanted to see whether the brothers would go back, and leave poor Benjamin to be a slave.

Judah then came nearer to Joseph, and began to beg for Benjamin with all his heart.

"Let me speak a word to my lord," said he, "and do not be angry with me, for I am as afraid of you as I am of the king. When we first came to buy corn, you asked us if we had a father and a brother, and we said, Yes; we had an old father, and a little brother that he loved very much indeed; and then you said that we must bring our brother to show you. Then we said we could not, because our father could not part with him; but you said we must bring him. So when we went back to our father, we told him what you had said, but he would not let Benjamin go. 'No,' said he, 'I had a dear child that I think was eaten up by a lion or a bear; if I let Benjamin go, perhaps some harm will happen to him, and then I shall die of grief, and these gray hairs will go down with sorrow to the grave.'

Then I promised my father that I would take care of Benjamin. I cannot go home without him. If I were to go back without Benjamin, we should see our father die. Let me be your slave instead of Benjamin, and let him go home to his father: for I could not bear to see my father die of grief."

Was it not kind in Judah to say this?

Now Joseph saw that Judah did indeed love Benjamin and his old father.

Now Joseph would tell his brothers who he was, and would tell them that he had forgiven them.

Joseph felt ready to burst into tears, yet he did not go out of the room to weep as he had done before; but he said to all his servants, "Go out of the room," and Joseph was left alone with his brothers. He cried so loud, that all his servants heard him though they were not in the room.

At last he said, "I am Joseph. Is my father yet alive."

Were his brothers pleased? No, they were frightened;—they could not speak, and they dared not come near him.

Joseph did not wish to frighten them; he longed to put his arms round them and kiss them.

He saw that they were unhappy at the thoughts of their wickedness in having sold him; so he tried to comfort them.

"Do not grieve because you sold me," said Joseph; "God let you do it, that I might save corn to feed your children. I wish you all to come and live with me here. You must bring my old father with you, and your children and I will feed you all. Look at me and you will see that I am indeed your own brother Joseph. It is my mouth that speaks to you. Go and tell my father what fine things I have in Egypt, and bring him here to live with me."

This was the loving way in which Joseph spoke. Then he threw his arms around Benjamin's neck, and wept as he kissed him; and Benjamin wept too upon Joseph's neck. Afterwards Joseph kissed all his brothers, and wept as he kissed each; and then his brothers no more felt afraid of him, but began to talk to him. They saw Joseph had quite forgiven them, and that he loved them with all his heart. They could not have expected such kindness, and it made them the more sorry for their own wickedness.

You see that Joseph did not make his brothers happy till he found that they were really sorry, and had left off their wickedness.

How like is Joseph to Jesus Christ, who forgives us all our sins when we are really sorry! You remember how he forgave that poor woman, who washed his feet with her tears, and wiped them with the hairs of her head. She was sorry for all her sins, and Christ forgave her. My dear child, if you are sorry for your sins, Christ will forgive you.*

* Repent therefore, and be converted, that your sins may be blotted out."—Acts iii. 19

"Let him with whom the cup is found,
His blood to Joseph pay;
And let the rest as slaves be bound,
And here for ever stay."
These words the guiltless brethren said,
And on the ground each sack was spread.

"Not so," the servant straight replied,
"For this no *blood* shall flow!
But he who dar'd the cup to hide,
Shall into slavery go."
They searched the sacks that lay around,
In Benjamin's the cup is found.

How bitterly the brothers grieve!
What anguish they express!
Dear Benjamin they will not leave
Alone in his distress,
But with him to the city go,
And there unfold their tale of wo.

Now for the youth hear Judah plead!
"Long since, a favourite son
My father lost; his heart would bleed
To lose this youngest one.
Such grief would bring him to the grave:
Let me instead become a slave."

What generous love! Can this be he,
Whose heart was once like stone,
And Joseph's pangs unmov'd could see
When in the pit cast down?
What transport now sweet Joseph feels
His name no longer he conceals.

Strangers may not the scene behold
When Joseph says, with tears,
"I am the brother whom ye sold;—
Yet calm your rising fears."

And while each shares his fond embrace,
The voice of weeping fills the place.

With anguish sore their hearts must melt
  Who Joseph's kindness share,
To think they had so basely dealt
  With such a brother rare:
While each forgiving word they hear
Must make their crimes more black appear.

CHILD.

Yet one there is more lovely far
  Than aught on earth can be,
One brighter than the morning star,—
  Yes;—one who died for me;
And oft have I his grace refus'd,
  His name forgot, his love abus'd.

The more I of his goodness know,
  The deeper is my shame,
That I so little love should show
  To his most blessed name.
How great my wonder then will be,
When his bright face in heaven I see!

CHAPTER XIX.

JOSEPH, OR THE LONG LOST SON.

Gen. xlv. 16 to end; xlvi.; xlvii. 1—12; l.

BEFORE Joseph told his brothers who he was, he had sent the servants out of the room; yet he had sobbed so loud that the servants had heard, and soon they knew the reason why Joseph had sent them out. The servants were glad to hear that Joseph had found his brothers. Joseph had not told the people of Egypt of his brother's wickedness.

Pharaoh, the king, heard of the brothers being found: and he too was glad, for he loved Joseph.

He called Joseph, and said to him, "Your brothers must come and live near you, and you must send for your old father, and for all the little children; and they shall have the best food in all the land to eat. We will give them houses, fields, and gardens, and they shall live together. We must send wagons to bring the little children, their mothers, and your old father: but they need not bring their things, for we will give them everything they want."

You see how kind the king was.

Joseph got wagons with some beasts to draw them, and he gave his brothers some food to eat as they travelled home. He also made them some handsome presents, for Joseph was very rich. He gave them each two suits of clothes; but to Benjamin he gave five suits of clothes, besides a great deal of money. He sent a present to his father; ten asses that carried all kinds of good things; and ten asses more that carried a great deal of bread and meat for his father to eat by the way.

When all the things were ready, Joseph told his brothers to go to Canaan, and to come back quickly. He gave them one piece of advice before they went. "Take care," he said, "that you do not quarrel by the way."

They must have had a pleasant journey.

Old Jacob had been longing to see them, much fearing lest Benjamin should not come back safely. At last they came, and he saw that not one was missing.

They told him quickly the joyful news. "Joseph is alive: and he is the great lord that sells corn in the land of Egypt."

Perhaps you think Jacob was delighted; but no, he would not believe them.

"No," said he, "my son has long been dead."

"But we have seen him," said they.

"It cannot be true," said Jacob.

Then the brothers told him what Joseph had said, "He desires us all to come and live with him, and he sends for you."

Still Jacob could not believe them.

"Only come and see the wagons he has sent, and then you will believe us," said they.

So they took old Jacob to see the wagons, and when he saw them he did believe; and then he was glad.

"It is enough," said old Jacob. "Joseph, my son, is yet alive; I will go and see him before I die."

The brothers told their wives and their children that they must leave Canaan, and take a long journey. They got into their wagons, and set out.

Jacob was lame* and old, and he rode in a wagon, but the brothers were strong enough to walk. And they took their sheep and cows, and goats, and camels, and asses with them, and all their things. They had to travel a very long way. No doubt the little children were much pleased, for children are fond of making journeys.

At last they all came into the land of Egypt.

Long before they came to Joseph's house, they saw a fine chariot coming towards them. It was Joseph's. It stopped, and Joseph got out of it.

Old Jacob stepped out of his wagon. His hair was gray, his legs were weak, and he could hardly walk. Joseph was a fine and glorious lord. He ran to meet his father, and threw his arms around his neck; and then he wept for a long while.

The last time Joseph had kissed his father was, when he was a boy dressed in his pretty coat, and was going to look for his brothers to see how they did. How many sad days had Jacob spent since that time, in thinking of him! And now at last had found him again.

The brothers did not feel envious now, when they saw Jacob and Joseph folded in each other's arms.

"Now," said old Jacob, "let me die since I have seen your face, Joseph, once more."

Then Joseph said to his father and brothers, "I will go and tell Pharaoh that you are come."

So Joseph went to Pharaoh the king, and said,

* (Jacob) halted upon his thigh.—Gen. xxxii. 31.

"My father, and brothers, and their flocks, and all that they have, are come."

And then he brought five of his brothers, and showed them to Pharaoh. And Pharaoh said to them, "What is your employment?"

"We are shepherds; but there is no grass in Canaan for our sheep. Will you give us some fields where we can feed them?"

Pharaoh said that he would give them a great many fields, and that they might live there altogether, with their children and their flocks.

Joseph wished them to live all together, because the people in Egypt worshipped idols.

Joseph wished the king to see his dear old father: so he brought him in to the king. The king treated him with great respect, because Jacob was a very old man. Even kings should pay respect to old men.

Should not children pay great respect to an old man? When they see a grey-headed old man, they should be ready to wait upon him, and to do what he bids them.

Old Jacob lifted up his hands over Pharaoh's head, and prayed God to show him kindness. This was called blessing him. Jacob blessed Pharaoh, because he had been very good to his dear Joseph. Jacob must have loved Pharaoh very much.

Pharaoh said to Jacob, "How old are you?"

Jacob said, "I am one hundred and thirty years old, but I am not as old as my fathers were; and my life has been full of troubles."

Then Jacob blessed Pharaoh again, and went away to the place Pharaoh had given him to live in. There he lived, with all his children round him. Joseph did not live with him, but he often came to see him.

Jacob at last fell sick, and knew that he soon should die. He sent for all his sons, that he might bless them before he died. Jacob had been lame a long while, and now he was almost blind, and very weak, and sick.

When his sons came, he sat upon the bed, and called them one by one, that he might give a blessing to each. After he had blessed them, he said, "I am soon going to die; bury me in the cave in Canaan where Abraham my grandfather is buried, and Isaac my father." He said a great deal more, and at last he gathered up his feet into the bed, and died.

His spirit went to God, and he is still with him in heaven. His body will rise from the cave at the last day.

Joseph fell upon his father's face when he was dead, and wept upon him, and kissed him. Those gray hairs had not gone down in sorrow to the grave, for God had comforted Jacob before he died.

Joseph took his father's body to Canaan, to put it in the cave were Abraham and Isaac were. All the brothers went with Joseph, and a great many servants, and chariots, and horses. Afterwards they came back to Egypt.

A very sad thought came into the minds of the brothers. They said to each other, "Perhaps Joseph has only been so kind to us to please his father; perhaps he has not really forgiven us; and now perhaps he will punish us." So they sent a servant to Joseph, and told the servant to say to Joseph, "Your father, before he died, told us to beg you to forgive us our great wickedness. So pray forgive us."

When Joseph heard this message, he began to weep. Why did he weep? Because he was sorry that his brothers should think he could be so unkind to them. Soon the brothers came and fell down before him and seemed much afraid. Joseph said, "Fear not: it was wrong in you to sell me, yet God made it turn out for good; because when I was in Egypt I saved the corn, and so you were kept from dying of hunger. I will still feed you and your little children." He spoke very kindly to them, and comforted them.

Joseph lived to be a very old man, and at last he died.

This is the history of Joseph. He is now in heaven with his dear Lord Jesus Christ. Joseph forgave his brothers, and Christ has forgiven him; for Joseph committed sins, though they are not written down in the Bible.

You have heard the history of Abraham, Isaac, and Jacob. God loved them all three. Abraham was the grandfather, Isaac the father, and Jacob the son.

God had promised the land of Canaan to the children of Abraham, Isaac, and Jacob: that is, to their great-great-grandchildren. God would not forget that promise. But he had made them a better promise than that: he had promised them that Jesus Christ should one day be born into the world, and should save them from their sins.* Abraham, Isaac, and Jacob† often thought of that promise.‡

At last Christ did come, and now Christ is in heaven with Abraham, Isaac, and Jacob, as well as Abel, Noah, and Joseph, and all good men, whose sins Christ has forgiven.§

Oh, my dear children, may you be with them one day!

> Full twenty years are pass'd away,
> Yet Jacob still laments the day
>   He lost his dearest one.
> Nor evermore can hope to see
> That face of innocence and glee
>   Until this life is done.

* The Scripture preached before the gospel unto Abraham.—Gal. iii. 8.

† Jacob's dying ejaculation was, "I have waited for thy salvation, O Lord."—Gen. xlix. 18.

‡ These all died in faith, not having received the *promises*, but having seen them afar off, and were persuaded of them, and embraced them.—Heb. xi. 13

Jesus Christ was a minister of the circumcision for the *truth* of God to confirm the *promises* made unto the *fathers*.—Rom. xv. 8.

§ Ye are come unto mount Sion . . . to the *general* assembly and church of the first-born, whose names are written in heaven . . . to the spirits of just men made perfect.—Heb. xii. 22, 23.

Though nought can give his spirit ease,
One infant, cherish'd on his knees,
  Has sooth'd his bitter wo.
To part with him he gave consent—
Now trembles lest some accident
  Has laid his darling low.

How vain are all his fond alarms
Again he clasps him in his arms,
  And gazes on his face.
And hark! he hears a strange report
That Joseph lives, and in a court
  Maintains the highest place.

Yet can he not the news believe
Until his aged eyes perceive
  The things that Joseph sent.
Then Joseph's words to him are told:
He cries "I shall his face behold,
  And I shall die content."

Mothers, and babes, and maidens fair,
A joyful, numerous train, prepare
  With Jacob to proceed.
These in the wagons safely ride,
While men and striplings, by their side
  The flocks and cattle lead.

Now Canaan's mountains disappear,—
Lo! Joseph's chariot's drawing near,
  Which princely honours deck:
Before his father, Joseph bows,
His arms around him fondly throws,
  And weeps upon his neck.

Another name sweet Joseph bears,
Another garb indeed he wears,
  His *heart* no change has known;

True piety his youth adorn'd
When by his cruel brothers scorn'd,
  And in the pit cast down:

And still his father's God he fears,
His aged father still reveres
  And sinful ways abhors:
And by his words and actions shows,
With love his heart still overflows
  For God's most holy laws.

CHILD.

In early youth I would begin,
As Joseph did, to flee from sin,
  And God's commands obey:
And though, awhile, I may be sad,
My God at length will make me glad
  In heaven's eternal day.

CHAPTER XX.

MOSES, OR THE BASKET OF BULRUSHES.

Exod. iii. 11—10.

You have heard how Joseph and his brothers lived happily in Egypt for a long while. At last they grew old and died, but they left a great many children; and their children had a great many children; till at last there were hundreds and thousands of people. These people were the grandchildren of Jacob, and his great-grandchildren and their children.

Did you know that Jacob had two names?

His other name was Israel. It was a name that God had given him.

All the sons of Jacob were called the children of Israel, or the children of Jacob, and the grand-children of Jacob were called by this same name, "children of Israel." There were some men, and some women, and some children, and all of them together were called "children of Israel."

The grown-up people were called "children of Israel."

They did not live in Canaan, you remember; they had left Canaan, because no corn grew there for a long while; they lived in Egypt, and took care of their sheep. While the good king Pharaoh lived, they were very happy. At last he died, and there was another king of Egypt: he was called Pharaoh. You shall hear what he did, and then you shall tell me whether you think he was good.

He knew that the children of Israel had come from a great way off, and he said, "there are so many of them, perhaps they may some day fight against me with swords, and kill me and my servants. I will make them work hard, and I will try to kill them with hard work."

So he desired that they should make a great many bricks, and build very high walls. He sent some of his men to make them work hard.

The children of Israel were used to taking care of sheep, and that is a pleasant employment. Shepherds lead their flocks to the green fields, and by the side of the quiet waters, and they sit under the shade of a tree when the sun is hot. Is not this pleasant? But now the children of Israel were obliged to dig up the clay, and to make bricks, and to dry them in the sun; and if they did not make a great number of bricks, the men whom Pharaoh had sent, beat them. So now they were very unhappy: they often sighed, and groaned, and shed tears.

Yet all this hard work did not kill them; so the king thought of another plan. "He said Let every boy-baby be thrown into the river." He did not order the girl-babies to be drowned, because they would not be able to fight with swords when they grew up.

Whenever the king heard that one of the children of Israel had a little boy-baby, he sent his men to throw it into the river.

There was a very good woman, who had a little boy-baby; she was one of the children of Israel. This woman knew that God would take care of her child, and she prayed to God to take care of it. She hid her baby, so that Pharaoh's men could not find it. I do not know where she put it, but God taught her to hide it in a very safe place.

When the baby was three months old, she found that she could not hide him any more. What should she do with her baby?

You have heard of the great river of Egypt. Close by the river there grew a great many reeds and bulrushes, whch are like very high thick grass.

THE FINDING OF MOSES.

She took some bulrushes, and made them into a large basket. She wished to make a basket into which the water could not come; so she got some pitch, and covered the basket with pitch. Then she put her little baby inside, and took the basket in her arms. No one could tell what was in the basket.

She went to the river side, and laid the basket among the great rushes, close by the water. She knew that God would not let the child be killed, and so she left it, trusting in Him.

She had a little girl much older than the baby. This little girl was the baby's sister. She stood a great way off, to see what would become of her baby-brother. Soon she saw some ladies walking by the river-side. One of these ladies was king Pharaoh's daughter. She was a princess. The other ladies were her maids, and they were going with the princess to some place where she could bathe; (for Egypt is a very hot country, and people bathe in hot countries.)

The princess was looking at the rushes, when she saw something very strange peeping out amongst them. When she saw it, she said to one of her maids, "Go and see what that is." So the maid went, and found the basket. She took it up and brought it to the princess. The princess opened the basket, and saw a sweet babe. It was fair and lovely.*

It began to weep. Poor infant! it was used to lie in its mother's arms, but now there was no one

* (Moses) was exceeding fair.—Acts vii. 20.

to feed it or to comfort it. The princess pitied the child. She had heard of how her father had desired that every baby should be thrown into the river, and she said, "I suppose this is the baby of one of the children of Israel." She did not wish it to be thrown into the river.

The baby's sister had come nearer, and had seen what the princess had done. She saw that the princess pitied it; so she said, "If you want a nurse, I could find you one who would nurse the child for you." The princess said, "Go."

Whom did she call? The baby's mother. When she was come, the princess said to her, "Take this child, and nurse it for me, and I will give you wages."

How glad the mother was to take care of it! She saw that God had heard her prayers, and saved her child from being drowned.

The mother could teach it about God as soon as he could understand. But she was not allowed to keep it always. When it was a big child, the princess sent for it to come and live with her, and she called it her son. She gave it a name. "I shall call it 'Moses,'" she said; which means, "drawn out," for he was drawn out of the water.

The princess lived in a fine house, and had a great many servants. Moses had beautiful clothes, nice things to eat, and servants to wait upon him. He had no hard work to do: yet he was not idle, but learned a great many things. The princess told wise men to teach him.

He knew the names of the stars; the names of the beasts, birds, and plants. He learned about all these things, and grew very wise. One thing these wise men could not teach him—even about God, for they worshipped idols. Yet Moses did know about God, for his father and mother knew the true God, and, when he was little, Moses lived with them. Of all the things Moses knew this was the best. He was wiser than all the men in Egypt, for he knew the true God.

He was brave as well as wise, and the people in Egypt praised him, and paid him respect. Was Moses happy? No; and I will tell you why in the next lesson.

"My child I can no longer hide thee:
So to my God alone confide thee."
Thus spake a mother, broken-hearted
As from her darling child she parted.

Once more with tenderness embracing
And in an ark the infant placing,
She to the river's side conveyed it,
And 'mong the flags in secret laid it.

The princess near her course is bending,
A train of maids her steps attending.
She cries, "What is it lying yonder?"
Then views the curious ark with wonder.

Within it lies a little creature,
Of fairest form and lovely feature;—
Behold, the Hebrew babe is weeping,
It needs a mother's tender keeping.

With pity mov'd, great Pharaoh's daughter
Resolves to save the child from slaughter;

To her kind heart its tears endear it.
And now she seeks a nurse to rear it.

A little maid has watched her brother;
She runs and tells the baby's mother,
Whom for its nurse the princess chooses,
Nor she the office sweet refuses.

Oh! who can tell the mother's pleasure,
Again to find her infant treasure!
Again beneath her roof behold it,
Again within her arms enfold it

Nor will she lose this precious season
To teach him many a holy lesson;
But use her every fond endeavour
To make him serve the Lord for ever.

Soon in a palace gay residing,
And in a heathen court abiding,
And every earthly good possessing,
He chiefly craves a heavenly blessing.

CHAPTER XXI.

MOSES, OR THE PIOUS CHOICE.

Exod. ii. 11—15.

I HAVE told you how very hard the poor children of Israel worked, in making bricks. When Moses was grown to be a man, this thought came into his mind;—"I live in a fine house, and am as great as a prince. I have no work to do; but my poor cousins, the children of Israel, they are working like slaves. Cruel men are beating them. Cannot I help them?" This thought made him sad.

Do you remember the promise God made to Abraham about his great-great-grandchildren? These children of Israel were the great-great-grandchildren of Abraham.

Abraham's child was called Isaac: Abraham's grandchild was Jacob; and Abraham's great-grandchildren, were Joseph and his brothers. Now Joseph's children were Abraham's great-great-grandchildren. and their children were his great-great-great-grandchildren. The children of Israel called Abraham their great-great-great-grandfather; only they had never seen him; he died before they were born.

You, my little child, have a great-great-grandfather. I do not know what his name was, but I know he has been dead a long while. If he were alive he would call you his great-great-grandchild.

I am now going to tell you about these great-great-grandchildren of Abraham, and Isaac, and Jacob, and about their children, and their children; and I shall always call them the children of Israel."

What promise had God made to Abraham about them? He had said that they should live in the land of Canaan—that sweet land, full of hills and rivers, grass and flowers, sheep and cows, milk and honey. God had said to Abraham, " I will give this land to your children." Not to Isaac, but to his great-great-great-great-grandchildren and to their children, and to their children.

Moses had heard of this promise; perhaps his mother told him of it. He had heard how he had been saved from being drowned when he was a little baby, and he believed that God would let him bring the children of Israel into Canaan. He wished to save them from being slaves among the wicked people of Egypt, and to make them happy in that pleasant land of Canaan. It was kind in Moses to wish to help the poor children of Israel.

Moses left the king's fine house and all his fine things, and he went to the place where the poor Israelites were working hard. (The children of Israel were sometimes called Israelites.)

He wished to see whether they remembered God's promise to Abraham, and whether they wished to go to Canaan.

When Moses came to the place in Egypt where the children of Israel were working, how sad was the sight he saw! They were labouring in the heat of the sun. They worked from morning to night. They dug up the clay to make bricks:—that was hard work. When they made the bricks, they put them in heaps to dry in the sun. Then they carried them to build the great walls for Pharaoh.

They were forced to make a great many bricks, and the cruel men that Pharaoh had sent, beat them when they were tired. They groaned and cried, but still they were made to do their tasks.

For the men set them a task; not such a little task as you have to do, but a great task. The men said, "You must make so many bricks." I do not know how many they told them to make, but a great many. If they did not do their task, the men would beat them.

It is a sad thing to be a slave. Did you ever hear this hymn?—

"I was not born a little slave
To labour in the sun,
And wish I were but in my grave,
And all my labour done."

Moses was very sorry to see how the poor children of Israel were treated.

One day he saw one of the task-masters (the cruel men were called task-masters) beating one of the children of Israel. Moses could not bear to see the poor slaves treated so cruelly. Moses looked to see whether there were any more task-masters near;—he saw no one. So he killed the task-master, and then dug a hole in the ground, and covered it over with the earth.

Do you think it was wrong in Moses to kill the task-master? It is very wicked to kill people, for God has commanded people not to kill each other. But God may have people killed if he chooses.

Moses had been sent by God to kill this wicked man, that he might show the poor Israelites that he was come from God to make them happy. So it was *not* wrong in Moses to kill the man, because God had sent him to do it.*

One of the Israelites saw him, and soon king Pharaoh heard of it, and Pharaoh was very angry and tried to find Moses, that he might have him killed. So Moses was obliged to go into a country a great way off, where the king could not find him. I will tell you another time what happened to Moses in that country. God loved Moses and took care of him wherever he went.

Moses might have lived always in a fine house, aud ridden in a chariot, and had many servants; but you see how much he loved the poor children of Israel. Do you not think that he was like the Lord Jesus, who left his throne in heaven to save us from going to hell?

Moses wished to please God more than to be called the son of Pharaoh's daughter.† He knew that God loved the children of Israel, and he knew that God would one day help him to take them into Canaan.*

"In vain for me are tables spread
  With costly meats and wine,
In vain upon a silken bed
  At noon-day I recline;—

For he supposed his brethren would have understood how that God by his hand would deliver them.—Acts vii. 25.

† By faith Moses, when he was come to years, refused to be called the son of Pharaoh's daughter; choosing rather to suffer affliction *with the people of God*, than to enjoy the pleasures of sin for a season; esteeming the *reproach* of Christ greater riches than the treasures of Egypt.—Heb. xi. 24—26.

"In vain on prancing coursers mount,
In warlike chariots ride;
Treasures of gold and silver count,
In palaces abide;—

"In vain am I for learning famed,
For courage and for strength;
And, son of Pharaoh's daughter named
May wear a crown at length;

"In slavery my brethren groan,
And eat their bread with tears;
Beneath a cruel master's frown
They spend their bitter years.

"Yet God our father Abraham bless'd,
And promis'd to bestow
Upon his seed a land of rest,
Where milk and honey flow.

"O! willingly would I forsake
This court and palace fair,
The glorious work to undertake
Of leading Israel there.

"O! happy day when we should see
The hills our fathers trod,
And, as our numerous family,
Worship our fathers' God."

CHAPTER XXII.

MOSES, OR THE BURNING BUSH.

Exod. ii. 16, to end; iii.; iv.

MOSES was grieved to leave the poor children of Israel groaning in Egypt; but he was forced to hide himself from Pharaoh.

He took nothing with him on his journey;—no servant, no ass! But God was with him. Though he could not see him, Moses knew he was near him, and this was his comfort.

At last Moses came to a place where there was much grass, and a great many sheep. Here, also, there was a well, and Moses sat down by the side of it; for he had taken a long journey.

He had no house, no bed, and no friend. He was like Jesus, who had nowhere to lay his head. But you will see that God will take care of him.

Soon there came seven girls to the well. They were sisters, and they took care of their father's sheep. They brought their sheep with them to give them water. First they let down some pails, or buckets, into the well, and then poured the water into some great troughs that stood near. And the sheep drank out of the troughs. While they were doing this, some shepherds came to the well, and tried to drive them away, that their own sheep might drink water out of the troughs; but the poor girls had filled the troughs with water, and it would have been very unfair to have taken the water from their sheep. But the men were stronger than they were, and often behaved in this way to them.

Moses did not like to see weak people ill treated; and he was very strong; so he stood up, and would not let the shepherds send the girls away, but helped them to draw water for their sheep.

The poor girls thought that Moses was very kind, because he was only a stranger, and yet he had helped them.

When they came home to their father, he said, "How is it that you are come home so soon to-day?" And they said, "A stranger was by the well, and he would not let the shepherds drive us away, and he drew water for our sheep."

Then the father answered, "Where is the man? Call him, and ask him to come and eat bread with us." So the girls called Moses, and asked him to come to their house.

It was God who put it into the man's heart to be kind to Moses.

The old father asked Moses to live with him and his daughters; and Moses said he would. Moses took care of the old father's sheep, and he married one of the seven girls. Then the old father was called Moses' father-in-law; because he was the father of his wife.

Moses had once been a fine prince, and had ridden in a chariot; but now he led his sheep to eat grass among the green hills.

There was one thing that must have made Moses

sad. What was that? He knew that the children of Israel were still groaning at their hard work. Could he be happy while they were so miserable? You know that he could not, because Moses loved those poor people.

The children of Israel were indeed working hard. King Pharaoh had died; but there was another king Pharaoh as wicked as he had been.

At last the children of Israel cried to God to help them, and God heard their prayers; and he remembered the promise made to Abraham, and he determined to save them. Now you shall hear what God did to help them.

One day Moses was with the old father's sheep, among the high hills. He was quite alone. He looked up, and saw a bush on fire. He went on looking, and the bush was still burning, but was not more burnt away than at first. This surprised him very much, and he said, "I will go and look at the bush, and see why it is not burnt up."

He was just going up to it, when he heard some one speaking to him. The voice came out of the bush. Whose voice could it be? it was the voice of God, who said to him, "Moses, Moses!"

He answered, "Here am I."

Then God said, "Come not near this place, for I am here. I have heard the children of Israel crying to me in their trouble, and I remember that I promised Abraham that his children should live in Canaan, and I am going to send them to Canaan.

Moses, you must go to Pharaoh, and tell him to let them go." •

Was not this a hard thing for Moses to do? But God said, "*I will* be with you and help you."

Then Moses said, "But perhaps the children of Israel will not choose to come out of Egypt. They will say, 'We will not go with you, Moses; you are not speaking the truth; God has not really spoken to you.' What shall I do then?" said Moses.

Then God said that he would teach him to do wonderful things. God said, "What do you hold in your hand?"

Now Moses had a long stick in his hand, called a rod. He used to help his sheep to get out of holes with his rod, and when he climbed high hills, he leaned upon his rod. So when God said, "What do you hold in your hand?" Moses answered, "A rod."

"Throw it upon the ground," said the Lord. And Moses did so, and it was turned into a serpent. Moses was afraid of the serpent, and began to run away from it.

Then God said, "Take hold of it by the tail." So Moses took hold of it, and it was turned again into a rod.

God said to Moses, "When you go to Egypt, do this wonderful thing before the children of Israel, to show them that I have sent you; but if they will not believe you, do this thing, too, that I will show you. Put your hand into your bosom."

So Moses put in his hand, and then he drew it out, and it was leprous, that is, it was all covered over with white spots. What a frightful sight this was!

Then God said, "Put your hand in again;" and he put it in, and pulled it out again, and then it was as well as it was before.

Then God said to Moses, "If the children of Israel will not believe that I have really spoken to you, let them see you do this wonder."

"But," said Moses, "I cannot speak well; I do not know what words to say."

Then God told Moses that Aaron, his brother, should go with him, and speak for him. You have not heard of Aaron before. He could speak well, and he was a good man, and loved God.*

Moses went back to his father-in-law, and told him that he must go back to Egypt, and he took his wife, and his two little sons with him upon an ass.

As Moses was going to Egypt he met his brother Aaron, and Aaron was glad to see him and kissed him. Then Moses and Aaron went together to the land of Egypt.

They found the poor Israelites at their hard work, crying and groaning. Aaron said to them, "God has sent us to tell Pharaoh to let you go to

* Aaron, the saint of the Lord.—Ps. cvi. 16.

the land of Canaan." Then Aaron did the wonders that God had shown Moses when he spoke to him from the bush. You know what wonders I mean.

Did the people of Israel believe what Aaron said? Did they wish to go to the land of Canaan? Yes, they did; and they thanked God for having heard their prayers.

I have often told you my dear child, that God hears people's prayers. I hope that you, my dear child, will always pray to him when you are unhappy.

The children of Israel did believe, and they said, "We will go;" and they bowed their heads, and thanked the Lord for his goodness.

But Moses could not take them out of Egypt till Pharaoh had given him leave.

Moses no more in courts abides,
'Midst noisy mirth and strife;
Within a stranger's tent he hides
From those that seek his life;
The stranger's daughter for a wife obtains,
And in that distant land he long remains.

Unable Israel to redeem,
Now patiently he waits;
Watching his flock beside the stream,
On God he meditates;
On His great love to Abraham of old,
And on the glorious things to him foretold.

Lo! In the desert God appears,
Cloth'd in a robe of flame—

Bids Moses dry his brethren's tears,
And liberty proclaim.
A court he once forsook to serve his God,
Soon Egypt's king shall tremble at his rod.

CHAPTER XXIII.

MOSES, OR THE FIRST PLAGUES.

Ex. v.; vi.; vii.; viii.; ix. 1—12.

THE next day Moses and Aaron, and some of the children of Israel with them, went in to speak to king Pharaoh. He was a proud and wicked man, and he worshipped idols.

It was Aaron who spoke to Pharaoh. He said, "The Lord God desires you to let the children of Israel go."

Do you think Pharaoh did let them go? No; he spoke proudly, and said, "Who is the Lord, that I should obey his voice? I know not the Lord, neither will I let Israel go." This was his proud answer.

He was now more unkind than before to the children of Israel, and ordered the task-masters to make them work harder; so that the children of Israel cried still more bitterly.

As Moses and Aaron came out from king Pharaoh they saw some of the children of Israel waiting for them. These men said to Moses and Aaron, "You have only done us harm by asking

Pharaoh to let us go. He makes us work harder than ever."

It was ungrateful in the children of Israel to speak in this manner to Moses, who had tried to help them. Moses was very meek and gentle, and he did not answer angrily but he went and prayed to God, and asked God what he must do now.

God told him to go in to king Pharaoh, and to show him the wonder of the serpent. So Moses and Aaron went in. Moses said to Aaron, "Take this rod and throw it on the ground;" and Aaron threw it down, and it became a live serpent; then afterwards it was turned into a rod again.

Would Pharaoh now say he would let Israel go? No, he would not; his heart was very hard, and he cared for nothing.

So God told Moses to do another wonderful thing, and I will tell you what it was.

Moses and Aaron went early in the morning down to the side of the river, and waited there till Pharaoh came: for he came there very often to bathe. Then they said to him, "Because you would not do as God desired, and let Israel go, now you shall see what God can do."

Then Aaron took the rod, and lifted it up over the waters: and, in a moment the water was turned into blood.

When Pharaoh saw this wonder, did he say that he would let the people go? No, his heart was very hard, and he would not obey God. Pharaoh turned back, and went into his house, and would not obey God.

The people of Egypt had nothing to drink, for all the water in the ponds was turned into blood, and all the water in jugs, and basins, and cups, was turned into blood. The fish in the river died, and a very bad smell came from the river. The people dug holes in the ground to get water. The water was blood for a whole week.

As Pharaoh would not mind, God sent him another plague.

Aaron stretched out the rod, and frogs came running out of the river, and out of the ponds, hundreds and hundreds of frogs. They ran into the streets, and into the houses, and into the bed-rooms, and into the beds ; they went into kitchens, and got among the food ;—they went even into Pharaoh's house and into his bed.

Then Pharaoh called for Moses and Aaron, and said to them, "Pray to God to take away the frogs. I will tell the children of Israel to go."

Moses went and prayed to God, and God made all the frogs die, so that the people swept the dead frogs into heaps, and these heaps had a very bad smell.

But still Pharaoh said, "I will not let the people go."

So God sent another plague.

Aaron stretched out the rod, and turned all the dust into nasty little insects, that crawled over men and over the beasts; but Pharaoh would not mind this plague.

Then God sent swarms of flies, that came in at the windows, and spoiled everything, in doors and out of doors. But no flies came near the children of Israel.

Then Pharaoh said, "I will let the children of Israel go, if God will take away the flies." Then Moses prayed to God, and God took all the flies away, and did not even leave one. Then Pharaoh said, "I will not let the people go."

So another plague was sent.

The beasts fell very sick—the horses, and asses, the camels, the cows, and the sheep—and a great many of them died. Yet Pharaoh would not let the people go.

Afterwards God made a great many boils come upon all the men, and women, and children, but not upon the children of Israel, only upon Pharaoh's people. They were so sick that they could not stand: yet Pharaoh would not mind, for his heart grew harder and harder.

I have now told you of six plagues. Try and remember what they were.

1. Water turned into blood.
2. Frogs.
3. Small insects.
4. Flies.
5. Death of the beasts.
6. Boils.,

I shall soon tell you of some more plagues that God sent to Pharaoh.

God was much stronger than Pharaoh, and was able to make him do what he commanded him to do. Was it not very wicked in Pharaoh not to mind God? and was it not very foolish in Pharaoh not to mind so great a God?

God will punish everybody who does not obey his commands.

My dear children, God has given you many commands. He has told you not to tell lies, not to fall into passions, not to be unkind. I hope you will try to obey God's commands. For if you think in your heart as Pharaoh did, "Who is the Lord that I should obey his voice?"—will not God be very angry with you?

CHAPTER XXIV.

MOSES, OR THE LAST PLAGUES.

Ex. ix. 13.; x.; xi.; xii.

ONE morning, Moses and Aaron rose up very early and came to Pharaoh and said to him, "To-morrow God is going to rain great hailstones from the sky,—such hailstones as were never seen in Egypt before. They will kill all men and beasts that are out of doors. Therefore you must keep your cows, and horses, and asses, in the stables, or they will be killed."

A great many of the men of Egypt heard Moses and Aaron say this. Some of them believed their words. They kept their beasts in their stables, and told their servants to keep in doors. But some of the men who heard did not believe, and let their beasts remain in the fields, and their servants with them.

The next day Moses stretched out his rod towards the sky, and God sent thunder and hail, and fire which ran along the ground. It was a most *dreadful storm. Such a storm was never seen before.* The noise of the hailstones and of the thunder must have made every one tremble who heard it. But how glad those must have been who were in their houses! Many beasts and men were killed, the grass and corn were burned up by the fire, and the trees were broken. Yet there was no hail where the children of Israel were.

This storm frightened Pharaoh, and he sent for Moses and Aaron, and said, "I have sinned; only pray the Lord to send no more thunder and hail, and I will let the children of Israel go."

Moses said, "I will go out of the city, and I will stretch out my hands to God, and he will not send any more thunder and hail: but still I know you will not obey God yet."

So Moses went out of the city, for he did not fear the storm. Then he stretched out his hands, and God made the hail and thunder stop, and he made the rain leave off.

Did Pharaoh let Israel go? No; when he saw that the storm was over, he would not. All Pharaoh's servants were wicked too; for they did not wish him to let the Israelites go.

Then Moses and Aaron went to king Pharaoh again, and said, "God will now send locusts into your country."

What are locusts? They are insects about the size of a child's thumb. Thousands of them fly close together in the air, and they perch upon the trees, and eat up all the leaves and fruit.

Pharaoh and his servants were very angry when they heard that the locusts were coming, and they spoke roughly to Moses and Aaron, and drove them out of the house.

Moses stretched out the rod, and God made the wind blow very hard, and next day the wind blew a great number of locusts into Egypt. The locusts made the sky look black as the wind blew them along; but they did not stay in the air: they perched on the trees, and ate up the fruit that the hail had left—they covered the grass and ate it up, and they even came into the houses.

Pharaoh and his servants thought that they should soon have nothing to eat. Pharaoh sent quickly for Moses and Aaron. "I have sinned," he said, "against the Lord, and against you. Only forgive me this once, and pray to God to take away the locusts, and I will let Israel go."

So Moses prayed to the Lord. God sent another wind, and it blew the locusts away, and they fell into the sea, and there was not one locust left in Egypt.

But Pharaoh still said, "I will not let Israel go."

How sad it must have been to have walked in the fields after the locusts had been there! It was the pleasant spring, but it looked like winter. There were no leaves on the trees, there was no tender grass, all was bare as in winter. What misery had *Pharaoh's* wickedness brought upon the land!

The next time Moses did not tell Pharaoh what God was going to do. Moses stretched out his rod towards heaven, and in one moment God made it dark. It was darker than ever it is at night. There was not the least light, except where the children of Israel lived;—there it was quite light.

The people of Egypt were very much frightened. They were doing their work, or eating, or walking, when all at once this darkness came on. They stopped, and sat down in the place where they were, and never moved, night nor day. Now they had time to think of all their wickedness.

It was dark for three days and three nights, and then it grew light.

But was Pharaoh sorry for his wickedness? No; his heart was harder than ever. He said to Moses, "Get away, you shall never see my face again. If you come in to me any more, you shall die."

Then Moses said, "You shall see my face no more."

God spoke to Moses again, and said, "I am going to send another plague. At night I shall come into every house in Egypt, and kill the eldest son of every person. But this is what I desire the children of Israel to do. Let each man take a lamb, a lamb without spot, and kill it, and eat it that night with his family; and let him take the blood of the lamb, and put the blood outside the door, and when I pass I shall see the blood, and I will not kill the eldest son in that house. Let the people in the house stand round the table while they eat the lamb. Let them all be dressed ready for a journey.

So all the children of Israel killed young lambs, roasted them, and ate them at night. They stood round their tables with their staves in their hands. They ate some bread with the lamb, and some bitter herbs. They did not forget to put some blood on the posts of the door, for then they knew they were safe.

The men of Egypt went to bed that night as usual, but in the middle of the night the eldest son in each house died. No one saw God's angel enter in, but yet he did come. No bars nor bolts could keep him out; but when he saw the blood on the door, then he passed over the house.

What a dreadful cry the fathers and mothers made in Egypt when they found their eldest sons were dead! They rushed out of their houses weeping. "Our darling son is dead," said one. "And so is mine," said another. "And mine." "And mine." There never was such dreadful crying heard in Egypt before.

Even Pharaoh's eldest son was killed, as well as the sons of poor people. Pharaoh rose up at night, *and called for* Moses and Aaron, but it was dark, so that they did not see his face.

"Go," said Pharaoh, "and take the children of Israel with you; they may take their sheep and cows with them, and all that they have."

And all the men of Egypt begged the children of Israel to go away as fast as possible, for they were afraid that God would kill them all."

Then the Israelites said to the women of Egypt, "Do give us some gold and silver before we go."*

And they said, "We will give you what you want; only go."

The Israelites had done a great deal of work in Egypt, and it was right they should have some money given to them.

So they gave them a great many beautiful things to take with them.

The Israelites went away in a great hurry. They took their things just as they were. They put bread in their bags—they drove their sheep, cows, camels and asses, before them, and so they set out in the night.

There was a great crowd of people. More people than live in any great town, except London. No little child could have counted them.

* The word "borrow" might equally well be translated "ask for," according to the testimony of the best commentators.

So at last they came out of Egypt, where they had been slaves so long. God had remembered his promise to Abraham, and Abraham's children were on their way to the land of Canaan.

God said to Moses, "They must never forget my kindness in bringing them out of Egypt. They must eat a lamb every year, as they have done to-night. Eating the lamb shall be called eating the Feast of the Passover." Why was this supper called the Passover? Because God passed over the doors where the blood was seen.

Of whom does the lamb that each family killed, make you think? Of Jesus.

That lamb's blood saved the eldest son in the family from being killed: and Jesus' blood saves all people who love him from being punished in hell. How kind it was in Jesus to shed his blood for us! We ought never to forget his kindness.

Now count how many plagues God had sent to Pharaoh, and the people of Egypt.

1. Water turned into blood.
2. Frogs.
3. Small insects from the dust.
4. Flies.
5. Death of the beasts.
6. Boils.
7. Hail and thunder.
8. Locusts.
9. Darkness.
10. Death of the eldest sons.

What dreadful plagues these were! But there will be much worse plagues in hell.

I hope, dear children, that you will obey God, and *not* make him angry with you. You know why God does not send us such dreadful plagues now. Jesus is praying for us, and God is waiting, that we may repent.*

PLAGUE 1.

How crimson now that mighty flood,
  That late like silver shone;
How dreadful too those draughts of blood,
  In troughs of wood and stone!

PLAGUE 2.

What troops of frogs the room infest,
  And mount the royal bed,
Defile the food for Pharaoh drest,
  The bak'd meats, and the bread!

PLAGUE 3.

The dust that lay so thick around,
  Now stirs and seems alive;
On men and beasts vile insects bound,
  And constant torment give.

PLAGUE 4.

What swarms of odious flies appear,
  And settle on the walls;
Their hateful buzz the king can hear
  Within his palace halls.

PLAGUE 5.

The flocks and herds now droop and die,
  Beneath the murrain's power:
Upon the open fields they lie,
  While vultures fierce devour.

* God is long-suffering to us-ward, not willing that any should perish, but that all should come to repentance.—2 Pet. iii. 9.

PLAGUE 6.

See pain is mark'd on every brow:
Hear moans from every breast;
A painful boil has laid each low,
And robbed his flesh of rest.

PLAGUE 7.

Now loud the mighty thunderings sound;
Torrents of hail-stones fall:
While streams of fire along the ground
The stoutest hearts appal.

PLAGUE 8.

Driven before the eastern breeze,
A cloud obscures the air:
The locusts cover o'er the trees,
And leave the branches bare.

PLAGUE 9.

Lo, sudden darkness spreads around,
And every face conceals;
None leaves the spot where he is found;
O'er all such horrors steals.

PLAGUE 10.

Ten thousand doors wide open fly,
Though daylight long has fled;
Ten thousand frenzied parents cry
"My first born son is dead.'

At length our God the victory gains
O'er Pharaoh's stubborn heart;
At length poor Israel leave obtains
From Egypt to depart.

CHILD.

'Tis vain against that God to strive,
Who heaven and earth commands;

How can a feeble sinner live,
  Who falls into his hands!

O Lord! this stubborn pride remove,
  That would resist thy will,
And make me with a child-like love,
  Obey thy precepts still.

CHAPTER XXV.

MOSES, OR THE RED SEA.

Ex. xiii. 20; xiv.; xv. 22.

The children of Israel had begun their journey to Canaan. But they had to travel a long way before they could reach that pleasant place. How would they find their way?

God himself showed them the way. He went *before them* in a dark cloud. The cloud moved, and they moved after it. But a black cloud could not be seen at night, so at night God made the cloud shine like fire. In the day the cloud was a shade from the sun, and in the night the fire gave light to the Israelites.* When the cloud or the fire stopped, then Moses desired all the people to set up their tents on the ground. This was called "encamping."

And as soon as the cloud moved, the people

* He spreads a cloud for a covering, and fire to give light in the night.—Ps. cv. 39.

folded up their tents, and placed them on the backs of their camels and asses, and went on their journey.

The children of Israel went very fast till they came to the sea-side. Then the cloud stopped, and they set up their tents close by the sea. This sea was called the Red Sea. Perhaps you think that the water of this sea was red like blood: but the water was like other water, though it was called the Red Sea.

They had not been long in their tents, before they heard a great noise: it was a noise of wheels, and a noise of horses. They looked, and saw, a great way off, Pharaoh and a number of soldiers in chariots, and on horses. Pharaoh had been sorry that he had let them go, and he was coming after them to bring them back.

The Israelites were very much frightened. What could they do? They could not get over the sea, for they had no ships: yet, if they staid where they were, Pharaoh and his men would soon overtake them, and fight against them, and Pharaoh's men could fight far better than they could. What could they do? They cried to God to help them. This was right; but they did something else that was not right; they began to speak angrily to Moses. "Why have you brought us up out of Egypt? We would rather have died there than come here: for we shall certainly be killed."

It was ungrateful to say this to Moses: but he answered them meekly. "Do not be afraid: God will fight for you, and you shall never see the faces of Pharaoh and his men again.

Then Moses went and prayed to God: for Moses knew that God would save the children of Israel.

Then God said to Moses, "Lift up your rod over the sea, and I will make a dry path for the Israelites to walk upon."

So Moses lifted up his rod, and the waters obeyed him; and part of the waters were lifted up on one side, and part on the other, and seemed like two walls of water, while a dry path was seen between.

The Israelites walked in the path, and all their cattle with them. It was the evening when they began to cross the sea, and they were walking across all the night: yet it was not dark.

I will tell you why it was not dark. You know that the cloud in the sky shone brightly in the night, and gave light to the Israelites. But God did not choose that Pharaoh should see the light; so God made the bright cloud to move backward; and it stood in the sky between the Israelites and Pharaoh: the bright side was turned towards the Israelites, and the dark side towards Pharaoh, so the Israelites saw a bright light: but the armies of Pharaoh were in the dark, and they could not go fast because it was so dark: but the Israelites walked quickly along the dry path, and by the morning they got to the land that was on the other side of the sea. They had not yet got to Canaan, but they had got over the sea, and they were on their journey to Canaan.

Now I will tell you whether Pharaoh and his men got over the sea or not. When they came to the edge of the sea, they saw a dry path through the sea, and the walls of water on each side: so they went along the dry path. When they had gone about half way across the sea, and were hoping soon to overtake the Israelites, God looked at them through his cloud. Pharaoh and his men heard dreadful noises, and they were very much frightened. It was God who made them afraid.

They could not make their chariots go on, and they thought that God was going to help the Israelites to kill them: so they said to each other, "Let us turn back."

Ah! it was now too late; God was going to destroy those wicked men: they drove as fast as they could, that they might get out of the water, but it was too late; for the walls of water fell down and covered them all, and they lay like stones at the bottom of the sea.

This was the end of Pharaoh and of his wicked servants. The Israelites had got safely over to the other side of the sea. As soon as they got over, God had desired Moses to lift up his rod, and to make the walls of water fall down and cover the dry path. Moses had done as God told him; and so Pharaoh and his men, who were in the middle of the sea, had been drowned.

In the morning the Israelites heard no sound of chariot-wheels coming after them, but they saw some of the dead bodies of Pharaoh's men lying on the edge of the sea: for the sea, which moves up and down, had tossed them upon the land.

Now the Israelites saw that the cruel men could hurt them no more: God had punished them for their wickedness, and had saved the poor children of Abraham as he had promised.

This was a happy morning for the Israelites. They thanked God for his goodness in saving them, and they sang together a beautiful song of praise.

The song began with these words: "I will sing unto the Lord, for he hath triumphed gloriously: the horse and his rider hath he thrown into the sea." This sea was called the "Red Sea."

The women made sweet music, and sang these same words. Moses' sister Miriam, who had watched him when a baby, played the music, and the women sang with her.

How pleasant it must have been to have seen the poor Israelites singing and rejoicing! A little while before they had been working hard in the sun, they had been beaten by cruel men, and had cried and groaned: now they were slaves no more, but they were on their way to a sweet land, where they might live happily.

Dear children, there is a sweeter land than Canaan. I hope we shall live there some day. Ought not we to praise God for telling us how we may get to that sweet land? God will help you, dear children, to get there, if you ask him very often. Satan, you know, is trying to get your souls: but God is stronger than Satan. God did not let Pharaoh hurt the Israelites, and God can prevent Satan hurting you.*

In deepest gloom of darkest night,
Between two walls of wondrous height,
Pharaoh, with all his men of might,
　　Poor Israel's host pursue.
The wind is high—the path is dry,
Horsemen and chariots swiftly fly:
"We'll overtake," they loudly cry,
　　"And kill that slavish crew."*

But sudden—drag their chariot-wheels,
A sudden horror o'er them steals,
While God on high his wrath reveals
　　From yonder fiery cloud.
The lightnings play—the thunders roar,
The skies a mighty torrent pour:‡
Were e'er such lightnings known before,
　　Or thunderings so loud?

The sound, the sight, o'erwhelm with fright,
Horsemen and chariots take to flight.
"Does not their God for Israel fight?"
　　The horsemen trembling cry.

* The God of peace shall bruise Satan under your feet shortly.—Rom. xvi. 20.

† The enemy said, I will draw my sword, my hand shall *destroy* them.—Ex. xv. 9.

‡ The 77th Psalm refers to the passage across the Red Sea, and thus describes the storm attending Pharaoh's destruction: "The clouds poured out water: the skies sent out a sound: thine arrows went abroad. The voice of thy thunder was in the heaven: the lightnings lightened the world: the earth trembled and shook."

But while with furious speed they go,
God makes the western wind to blow,*
And o'er their heads the waters flow:
    Like stones the horsemen lie.

Beneath the deep their bodies sleep—
And they shall rise to wail and weep,
And God upon their heads shall heap
    Hailstones and coals of fire.
What piercing cries shall rend the skies,
When *all* who were God's enemies,
Shall meet the Judge's angry eyes,
    Flashing with terrors dire!

How vain to try from him to fly,
Who made the sea, the earth and sky,
Whose arm can reach the mountains high,
    And deepest pits beneath!†
How vain to try from him to fly,
Who can all secret things descry,
Whose power no angels dare defy,
    Whose *word* can blast with death!

* Thou didst blow with thy wind, the sea covered them.—Ex. xv. 10. As it was by an *eastern* wind that the sea was made to go back, (Ex. xiv 21,) it is evident that it was by a *western* wind it was made to overwhelm the enemy: which fact is proved by the circumstance of the dead bodies of the Egyptians being washed upon the *eastern* shore the following morning.—Ex. xiv. 30.

† Though they dig into hell, thence shall my hand take them: though they climb up to heaven, thence will I bring them down; and though they hide themselves in the top of Carmel, I will search, and take them out thence.—Amos ix. 2, 3.

CHAPTER XXVI.

MOSES, OR THE MANNA AND THE ROCK.

Ex. xvi.; xvii. 1—7.

The children of Israel were very glad that they had got away from their cruel masters. Now they had no hard work to do, and they had a kind master, even Moses. Ought they not to have been good and happy?

They were now in a very large wilderness. I will tell you what sort of a place this wilderness was. There were no men nor houses in it; but there were lions and bears, who roared and howled;* and there were serpents which bite, and scorpions which sting; there were no rivers nor brooks, but there were high hills, and dark pits. There were scarcely any fruit-trees or corn-fields, so that there was very little to eat:† and the Israelites could not sow corn, nor plant fruit-trees, because they were travelling. What could the poor Israelites do for food?

There was such a number of people that they wanted a great deal of food to feed them. They

* The waste-howling wilderness.—Deut. xxxii. 10.

† That great and terrible wilderness, wherein were fiery serpents and scorpions, and drought, where there was no water.—Deut. viii. 15. Where is the Lord that led us through the wilderness, through a land of deserts and of pits, through a land of drought and of the shadow of death, through a land that no man passed through, and where no man dwelt?—Jer. ii. 6.

had taken a little bread with them in their bags, when they had left Egypt; but they ate it up very soon.

What ought they to do now? They ought to pray to God. He loved them, and would not let them starve. But these naughty Israelites began to grumble. They went to Moses and Aaron, and said, "We wish we had died in Egypt. At least we there had bread and meat, as much as we could eat: but now we shall be starved. You have only brought us out of Egypt to kill us."

How ungrateful they were to Moses and to God!

Yet Moses did not answer roughly. He knew that God heard their wicked words: and God did hear them. God called to Moses, and said, "I have heard them, and I will feed them."

Did they deserve to be fed? O no! How do you think God would feed them? He would rain down bread from heaven. Was not this kind?

Next morning the children of Israel, when they looked out at their tent doors, saw the ground was white. They looked to see what made the ground white, and they saw little round white things on the ground. They said to each other, "What can this be? We never saw anything like it before."

Then Moses said, "This is the bread that God has sent you from heaven; gather it, and take it to your tents."

So all the men got jugs, and baskets, and gathered the manna for themselves, for their wives, and for their little children: and there was enough for them all: not too much, nor too little, but just enough. They tasted it, and found it was as sweet as honey, and they called it "manna."

Then they took it home, and their wives cooked it for dinner: they crumbled it, and baked it, and made it into cakes.* They had manna for breakfast, for dinner, and for supper; nothing but manna. It was very nice, and wholesome. It was more fit for angels than for men to eat, because it came from heaven,† and did not grow out of the ground, as corn does. God sent it very early, before it was light, and every one was obliged to get up early to gather it, because, when the sun was hot it melted away, so that if the Israelites did not get up soon, they had no food.

Moses said to them, "Do not save any of the manna, for God will send you some every day. If it is all gone at night, do not be afraid: trust God. He will send you more.

But some of the people chose to save some of the manna. They were disobedient and ungrateful. They looked at their manna next morning, but it was full of worms. They could not eat it,

* And the people went about and gathered it, and ground it in mills, or beat it in a mortar, and baked it in pans, and made cakes of it.—Num. xi. 8.

† He had rained down manna upon them to eat, and had given them of the corn of heaven. Man did eat angels' food.—Ps. lxxviii. 24, 25.

but were obliged to throw it away. How foolish it is not to mind what God says!

Soon afterwards the people had no water to drink. There was no river in the wilderness, and very few wells, or ponds. Do you think God would let them die of thirst?

These naughty Israelites thought God would. So they went to Moses, and spoke very angrily.

"Why did you bring us up out of Egypt? You mean to kill us, and our little children, and our cattle with thirst."

They were so very angry, that Moses thought they would soon throw great stones at him and kill him. Yet Moses did not answer, but began to pray to God, "What shall I do for these people?" said Moses.

Then God said to Moses, "Take your rod, and go up a hill, and let some of the people go with you. Then, when you are come to a high place close by a rock, strike the rock, and water shall come out."

So Moses took some people with him, and struck the rock, and water came running out.

A rock is a hard dry place, yet God made water come out of it. The water came running down. The people at the bottom of the hill saw the water running down like a river, and flowing upon the dry ground.

What a pleasant sight for the thirsty people! Their mouths were dry, and their tongues were stiff, their throats burning; but now they might stoop down and drink, or they might fill their jugs with water. The poor cows, and sheep, and asses, ran to the water to drink.

You see how kind God had been to them in their distress. Ought they not to trust him always—and to feel sure that he would help them?

God is very kind to you, dear children. You ought never to murmur like the Israelites, but to thank and praise God.

Israel must cross the desert wild,
Where craggy rocks on rocks are piled;
No waters flow,
No flowers grow
Upon that barren ground.
The pits are deep,
The scorpions creep,
And wild beasts howl around.

But Israel need no evil fear,
For Israel's God is ever near.
His cloud by day
Points out the way,
And shades them from the heat:
In robes of light
God shines at night,
And guides their wandering feet.

What though no golden ears of corn
The barren wilderness adorn,
Yet angels bread
From heaven is shed,
Like dew upon the ground:
Ten thousands eat
This manna sweet,
And still enough is found.

What though no river winds its way
Where travellers may their thirst allay,
At Moses' touch
The waters gush
Fast from the rock they stream;
And rush, and roar,
As down they pour,
And like a river seem.

CHILD.

They say this world's a vale of tears,
(Although so pleasant it appears,)
That all on earth
Is little worth,
And cannot make us blest:
That pleasures fly,
Friends droop and die,
And sickness breaks our rest.

So let them say, for well I know,
From God the sweetest pleasures flow,
And he could be
A friend to me,
Should all besides depart:
In sickness soothe
My pillow smooth,
And cheer my fainting heart.

While through this world my footsteps stray,
This blessed God shall be my stay,
My manna sweet,
My shade from heat,
My light in deepest gloom·
His love shall flow
Where'er I go,
Until I reach the tomb.

CHAPTER XXVII.

MOSES, OR MOUNT SINAI.

Gen. xix.; xx.; xxiv.; xxxi. 18.

The Israelites went on travelling through the wilderness. The wilderness was very large, and it would be a long while before they could get to Canaan.

They soon came to a very high mountain. It was called Mount Sinai. It was the same mountain where Moses had seen the bush on fire when he was keeping his sheep. Now he had brought the children of Israel to that very place where God first had spoken to him.

The Israelites placed their tents near the bottom of the mountain; for the cloud had stopped, and so the Israelites knew that they ought to wait in that place.

God told Moses to come up to the top of the mountain, for he had something to say to him. So Moses went up. Then God said to him, "You see how kind I have been to the children of Israel in bringing them out of Egypt: go down and ask them whether they will do what I desire them; for if they will, they shall always be my own dear people."

So Moses went down and asked them if they would obey God. And they said, "Yes, we will do all that the Lord tells us."

Then Moses went up to the top of the mountain again, and told God what the people had said. "They say we will do all that you command them."

Then God said, "I am now going to let the people hear my voice, and they shall see me speaking to you Moses. Go down and tell them to get ready."

So Moses went down and said, "In three days you will hear God's voice, and see him in a cloud at the top of the mount. Get ready and wash your clothes."

So the people washed their clothes, that they might all stand in clean white clothes before the Lord. Moses desired men to put rails all round the mount, that no one might go up the mount, or even touch it. No, even the sheep must not eat the grass upon that mount, for it was the mount of God.

In three days, early in the morning, the people heard a loud voice, and they all trembled. Moses desired them to come out of their tents, and to look upon God.

What a dreadful sight they saw! The mountain was shaking and moving up and down. On the top a great fire was seen, and a thick cloud, and such a smoke went up, as filled the sky with blackness and darkness. There were thunders and lightnings, and a sound came out of the fire. It was like the sound of a trumpet, and every moment it grew louder and louder. Even Moses himself was frightened, and said, " I tremble, and am afraid."*

The Lord said to Moses, " Come up to me on the top of the mount."

So Moses went up, and all the people saw him go. He went upon the shaking mount, and into the midst of the smoke.

When Moses came up, God said to him, (but God did not speak very loud,) " Go tell the people not to come up after you, for they must not come up this mountain."

And Moses said, " I have put rails round the mount."

But still God said, " Go and tell them not to come near," for God knew how bold and disobedient the people were.

So Moses went down and said, " Do not dare to touch the mountain or you will be killed."

Then God spoke very loud indeed, so that all the people heard; and as they heard, they trembled. Could you have seen that mountain, you would not wonder that they trembled as they stood round it.

What did God say in that loud voice? You have often heard the words at church. These are the words that God said: " I am the Lord thy God, that brought thee out of the land of Egypt, out of the house of bondage, (*or from the place where you were slaves.*)

* And so terrible was the sight, that Moses said, " I exceedingly fear and quake.' —Heb. xii. 21.

I. Thou snall have no other gods before me.

II. Thou shalt not make images, and worship them, (*such things are called idols.*)

III. Thou shalt not take the name of the Lord thy God in vain.

IV. Remember the Sabbath day to keep it holy, because in it God rested from his works.

V. Honour thy father and thy mother.

VI. Thou shalt not kill.

VII. Thou shalt not commit adultery, (*that is, a man must not take away another man's wife nor must a woman go away from her husband, and have another husband.*)

VIII. Thou shalt not steal.

IX. Thou shalt not bear false witness against thy neighbor, (*that is, no one may tell lies of other people.*)

X. Thou shalt not covet," (*or wish for other people's things.*)

This was what God said on the mount, and then he said no more.

The people were glad when God had left off speaking, for they could not bear the sound of that terrible voice; but while he was speaking, they had gone further and farther away.

Soon they came to Moses, and they said to him, "Ask God never to let us hear his voice again, it frightens us so much. We wish God to tell everything to you, Moses, and you can tell us what he says."

So Moses went up again to the dark cloud at the

top of the mount, and told God what the people had said. "They do not wish to hear thee speak to them again," said Moses.

And God said they have done well in not wishing to hear my voice. I shall speak to you, and you shall tell them; and O that they would obey me, and that I might bless them always!"*

You see that God wished the people to be good and happy; but he knew that they did not love him in their hearts.

Moses did really love God. God talked to him a great deal. God told Moses to come up to him quite alone, and to stay with him at the top of the mountain; and so Moses stayed with God forty days and forty nights, and all that time he neither ate bread nor drank water; but God kept him alive, and talked to him out of the thick cloud.

At the end of the time God gave Moses a book. What kind of book? It was not made of paper like the books you have seen. It was made of stone. It had only two leaves, and on those leaves very little writing. God had made this stone book, and God had written in it with his own finger.

You would like to know what was written in it. God had written in it all the words he had spoken in the loud voice from the cloud. The ten things God had told the Israelites, are called the Ten Commandments.

He had written them down that Moses might

* Deut. v. 22—29.

read them to the children of Israel, so that they might never forget God's commandments.

Neither ought we to forget God's commandments. They are written up in some churches, that we *may read them.* Did you ever see them? I should like you, my dear children, to learn these commandments; and I will tell you the meaning of them over again.

One of these commandments was, "Thou shalt have no other gods but me." God wished the Israelites to love him better than any thing else. But they did not. We shall hear of their wickedness. We ought to love God better than everything else; for there is no one so kind and so good as God.

O God, how terrible wert thou,
When from the mountain's burning brow
    Thy voice was heard!
Thunders and lightnings with thee came,
And thickest smoke and raging flame
    Around appeared.

Well might each heart with terror thrill,
As loud—more loud—and louder still
    The trumpet grew.
Well might a thousand lips implore
To hear thine awful voice no more,
    Lest death ensue.

And yet the voice they could not bear
Is heard above,—by angels fair,
    With great delight;
When Adam dwelt in Eden's ground,
He heard that voice, nor did the sound
    His soul affright.

But when thy law he disobey'd,
For fear of thee—in deepest shade
He hid his head.
Thy thunderings' roar, and lightnings' blaze,
Would thus no righteous soul amaze,
Nor fill with dread.

And Israel too had broke thy law—
So trembled when they heard and saw
Thy dreadful power :
The God who made the thunders roll,
They knew could plunge each sinful soul
Where flames devour.

And have I not deserved to die?
How shall I dare to venture nigh
Thine awful throne!
My sins would fill my soul with dread,
Did not the blood that Jesus shed,
For all atone.

CHAPTER XXVIII

MOSES, OR THE GOLDEN CALF.

Ex. xxxii.

Moses stayed in the mount forty days and forty nights. How did the Israelites behave when he was gone?

At first they behaved well, but at last they grew tired of waiting—they grew impatient. They wanted to go on to Canaan quickly, but the cloud stopped at the top of the mountain, and they were not allowed to go on unless it moved, and unless Moses told them to move: and now Moses was on the top of the mountain, they began to think he would never come back; so they went to Aaron, and said to him, "Make us some gods to go before us, for we do not know what is become of Moses."

How wicked a thing to ask! But you know they had lived in Egypt, where they had seen people worship idols, and they had learned to do the same.

Aaron was afraid that they would kill him, if he did not make an image to please them. So he said, "Bring me your gold earrings." And the people brought him their golden earrings.

How did they get so many golden things?

The women of Egypt had given them gold before they set out on their journey.

Aaron melted all the earrings in the fire; then, when the gold was soft, he took a knife and cut it into an image. He made it in the shape of a calf. The people in Egypt worshipped calves.

As soon as the Israelites saw it they began to praise it, and say, "This is he who brought us out of Egypt." Then Aaron put it on a high place, and built an altar before it, and said that they would have a great feast the next day.

The next day they rose up early. They spent the day in worshipping the calf. They took their lambs and goats, and offered them on the altar of sacrifices to the calf, and then rose up to sing ana dance, all the while praising the calf.

You remember that they had promised a little while ago always to obey God, but they did not keep their promise. One of the ten commandments was, "Thou shalt not make an image, and bow down to it." How soon they broke that commandment!

Moses was at the top of the mountain talking with God. He did not know what they were doing, but God knew: and he said to Moses, "Go down; the people you brought out of Egypt have made a golden calf, and are worshipping it. I am very angry with them, and I will kill them all; but I will save you, Moses, and your children."

Moses was grieved to hear that the Lord was angry, and he entreated God to forgive the people. "Remember," he said, "how you have brought them out of Egypt, and how you promised Abraham that you would bless his children." And the Lord heard Moses' prayer; and determined that he would not kill them all. How kind Moses was to pray for the people; How kind God was to say that he would not kill all the people!

Then Moses went quickly down the mount, with the book of stone in his hand. When he had almost come to the bottom of the mount, he heard the noise of singing, and he knew that it was the Israelites praising their calf. At last he came to the tents, and he saw the calf, and the people dancing round it, like mad or drunken people. It was a dreadful sight for Moses to see. He grew more angry still, and he threw down the stone book upon the ground, and broke it into pieces. The Israelites had broken God's laws, and Moses broke the book in his anger and his grief. Moses would not give that stone book to these wicked people.

Do you not think the people must have been afraid when they saw Moses again?

They had thought they should never have seen him again: but he had caught them in their wickedness.

He took the calf—(and no one tried to hinder him)—he threw it again in the fire: then afterwards he ground it into powder, and threw it into some water, and made the Israelites drink that bitter water.

Moses was very angry with Aaron for having made the calf. Moses said to him, "Why did you let the people be so wicked?"

Aaron said, "do not be angry with me: the people chose to be wicked, and they asked me to make the calf; I did it to please them."

This was a bad excuse. It was very wicked in Aaron to make the calf. We should not do wicked things, even when people ask us.

Moses told some of the men to take swords, and to kill a great many people; and they killed three thousand men with swords. And God made a great many other people fall very ill.

These were the punishments that God sent to

the wicked Israelites. They deserved to be killed for worshipping the golden calf; but God listened to Moses' prayer, and did not kill them all.

You have heard how the stone book was broken. God did not make a new one himself, but he told Moses to make a book of stone, and then God wrote the ten commandments in it, as he had done in the other book.

God called Moses up into the mountain again, and then God wrote the ten commandments in the stone book. God told Moses to stay alone with him on the mountain forty days and forty nights. God talked to Moses as friends talk to one another. He did not speak in that loud voice which had frightened the Israelites, nor did he make it thunder, and lighten, and smoke when he talked to Moses. Moses liked being with God upon the mountain. Why was not Moses afraid of God? Because God's Spirit was in him. Dear children, you will love God like a father, if God's holy Spirit is in you. God let Moses see some of his glorious brightness; but God would not let him see his face, because Moses would have died had he seen God's face. The angels and the people in heaven* see God's face, but men upon earth could not bear such brightness.

I will tell you soon what God said to Moses when he was alone with him on the mountain.

Moses ate no bread, and drank no water, while he was alone with God.

* They shall see his face.—Rev. xxii. 4.

At last Moses came down again to the people, with the stone book in his hand. This time the Israelites were not worshipping an image; they came up to Moses to speak to him; but when they looked at his face, they were afraid to come near him; even Aaron, Moses' brother, was afraid. What could the reason be?

The reason was, Moses' face shone like the sun, and they could not bear such brightness. And *what had made his face shine?*

He had been talking with God and looking upon his glory, and this had made his face so bright. For God is brighter than the sun, and the angels who look upon God are bright like him.

When Moses knew why the people could not come near him, he took a thick veil, and covered his face, and then he called them, for he wanted to tell them what God had said to him.

Then Aaron and the people came to him, and now they could look at him. Moses kept the veil on his face all the time he talked to them.

I hope, dear children, that your faces will one day shine bright in heaven.* If you love God now, I am sure one day you will see him in heaven, and then you will be like the angels.

Is that the conqueror's cry,
Or voice of those that fly?
It is the merry sound
Of those that dance around
  Some frightful idol god.

* And they that be wise shall shine as the brightness of the firmament.—Daniel xii. 3.

The feast was lately spread ;—
Their cheeks with wine are red ;—
They fling their robes away,
And sing, and dance, and play,
  And praise their idol god.

Can this the people be,
From Egypt just set free ?
Have they so soon forgot
The wonders for them wrought
  By their own fathers' God ?

O conduct mean and base !
Foolish, ungrateful race !
How can they thus reward
The goodness of the Lord,
  And serve an idol god ?

While I thus Israel blame,
Let me not do the same ;
O ne'er would I be found
Amidst the giddy round
  Of those who serve not God.

Whilst I remain on earth,
In dance, and song, and mirth,
My days I would not spend,
For fear I should offend
  My own All-gracious God.

CHAPTER XXIX.

MOSES, OR THE TABERNACLE.

Ex. xxxv.; xxxvi.; xvii.

Moses had been with God upon the mount a great many days. I have not told you what God was teaching him, but now you shall hear. God was showing him how to make a beautiful house.

Whose house was it to be? The house of God. God did not need a house, for his throne is in the sky; but he was so kind as to say that he would let the Israelites make him a house in the wilderness.

When Moses came down from the mount, he called all the people round him. He wanted to speak to them. He wore his veil over his face while he spoke.

He said first, "God desires you to do no work on the sabbath-day, but to worship him, and he is going to have a beautiful house made, where you can come and pray to him. Who will bring me things with which to make the house?

Had the children of Israel any beautiful things that they could bring to Moses?

You remember that the women of Egypt had given them a great deal of gold, and silver, and cloth and linen. They had made a calf with *some* of their gold, but they had a great deal more beside.

But do you think they *would* give these things to God?—or would they say, "We cannot spare our things; we mean to make fine clothes, and to make our tents look pretty inside?" Do you think they would part with their pretty things? Yes they would. They all went to their tents after Moses had spoken to them. They opened their boxes and their baskets, and they took out gold and silver rings and earrings, and they took out beautiful pieces of cloth; some were blue, some were purple, and some were scarlet; and a great deal of fine white linen, and skins of sheep and goats, and beautiful kinds of wood. They brought all these things to Moses. What a large heap there must have been!

Some of the rich men had beautiful shining stones, and sweet spices, and oil: and they brought them to Moses.

Moses was pleased to see that the people would give their things to God, and most of all he was glad that they liked to give them. They did not feel sorry when they gave them, but they were glad that they had something to give. If we feel sorry when we give things, God is not pleased.*

Who was to make the beautiful house? It was very hard to make such a beautiful house as God would choose to have.

Moses called the children of Israel, and said, "God has got two men very clever in cutting stones, in carving wood, and in making all kinds

* God loveth a cheerful giver.—2 Cor. ix. 7

of curious things, and he has told me their names."

Then Moses called these two men, and he gave them all the beautiful things, and said, "Now begin to make the house, and I shall tell you what you shall make." And Moses called every one to help them: and he told the two clever men to teach the others.

It is God who makes people clever: so that when people can make beautiful things, they should not be proud: but they should thank God.

So all the people began to work. The women spun blue, and purple, and scarlet thread and worsted. The men made the thread into linen and cloth: they cut the wood with saws and hammers; they melted the gold and silver in the fire, and then made altars, and candlesticks, and shovels, and tongs, and basins, and many other things. They worked hard for many months till all the things were finished.

I will now tell you what sort of a house God had told Moses to make.

It was not a house made of bricks nor stone; because this house would be moved from one place to another: so it was not fastened to the ground, but it was made like a tent and it could be moved very easily.

You never saw so large a tent as this was. It was as big as a very large room. It was called "The Tabernacle."

There were a great many boards that were placed upright on the ground, and close together.* These boards were the walls of the house; but there were no boards at the top; curtains were thrown over the house to cover the top. There was no door to the house, but a curtain hung down in front, and that curtain was instead of a door.

There was no floor to the house: green grass was the only floor.

The house was very beautiful; for the boards were covered with gold, and the curtains were blue, purple, and scarlet, and there were five posts of gold in front, over which a curtain hung down for the door, of which I told you before.

The house had two rooms inside. The first room was the largest. I will tell you about the beautiful things that were placed in it.

In the first room there were three very beautiful things.

1. In the middle an altar of gold; but no lamps were burned upon it, only sweet spices, which made the tabernacle smell most sweet. The burning spices were called "incense."

2. On one side there was a golden table, and on the table twelve loaves. They were called the shew-bread, or holy bread. There was fresh bread put there every sabbath-day.

* The mode of joining the boards may be explained to some children. Rings were placed in the boards, and long poles were run through these rings.

3. On the other side there was a golden candlestick with seven lamps. There was no window in the tabernacle, but these lamps made it light.

This room was very beautiful and sweet, but there was another room still more beautiful.

It was the inner room, on the other side of the curtain. There was a curtain between the big room and the little room. This curtain was instead of a door. It was called "The Veil."

In the little room there was a golden box, with golden angels on the top. This box was called "The Ark." Inside the box the book of stone was placed. But what made this room so glorious was, that God used to come down in his cloud, and fill this little room with his brightness.

The cloud rested between the golden angels on the top of the box.

The top of the box was called the mercy seat, because God sat there, and God is full of love and mercy. This little room was called "The Holy of Holies."

It had no window in it, and no candle, but yet it was light. The glory of God made it light, for God, you know, is brighter than the sun. What a sweet place this little room must have been! It makes me think of heaven, for there God lives, and there he shines. But heaven is not a little place. It is a very large place, and it will hold all the people who have loved God on earth, besides all the angels.

I will not tell you any more about the tabernacle

now: but I will write down the names of the things in the tabernacle. Can you remember what they were?

In the first room,

1. The golden altar.
2. The table of shew-bread.
3. The golden candlestick.

In the little room, or Holy of Holies, the Ark.

Where the angels' golden wings
O'er the ark together meet,
Sat enthroned the King of kings,
On his glorious mercy-seat.

Curtains all around were spread.
Shutting out the light of day:
Neither lamp nor candle shed,
In its stead their feeble ray.

Yet there shone a fairer light
Than this earth could e'er afford;
Can the sun be counted bright,
When compared with the Lord?

'Tis his face makes heaven so fair;
With fond rapture angels gaze,
Sweetest smiles for ever wear,
Joyful songs for ever raise.

The bright sun shall cease to shine,
Lamps and candles shall expire;
But the glorious face divine
Still shall bless the heavenly choir.*

Soon shall earthly pleasures die,
Like the candle's feeble flame;
God can brighter joys supply,
Through eternal years the same.

* A band of singers. The heavenly choir are saints and angels.

CHAPTER XXX.

MOSES, OR THE PRIESTS.

Ex. xxxviii.; xxxix.; xl.

I HAVE now told you what kind of a place the tabernacle was. I am now going to tell you of some things that were placed outside of it. You know that houses often have a garden round them. The tabernacle had no garden round it, but there was a large piece of ground near it, called the court: and there were posts round the court. These posts were placed at a little distance from each other, and curtains were hung between the posts: so there was a wall of curtains round the tabernacle.

In this court there were two things, of which I shall speak to you.

1. A brass altar.

This altar was very large. It was not like the little altar of gold inside the tabernacle. This altar was not for the burning of spices, but for the burning of beasts, such as sheep, goats, bulls, and calves. You know that God had desired people to offer beasts to him as sacrifices. Do you remember the reason? What promise had Jesus made to his Father a long, long while before? He had promised to die for men. God wished people always to remember this promise, so he told them to kill beasts, and to sprinkle their blood, and to burn their bodies. Abel, Noah, and Abraham offered sacrifices.

This brass altar was for the sacrifices.

The lamb was to be killed, and its blood would flow all round the altar, and the smoke of the burning would go up to the sky.

2. A brass basin was placed in the court. It was very large, and it was filled with water for people to wash in. I shall soon tell you who washed in this basin.

Who was to offer the sacrifices? Aaron. God said that Aaron should be the "High Priest." Aaron was to offer the sacrifices, to burn the incense, and to light the lamps of the candlestick.

God said that Aaron might go into the little room, the Holy of Holies; God would not allow any person but Aaron to go in there, and he only allowed him to go in once every year. Aaron might lift up the veil, and see the cloud upon the mercy-seat. Moses might go in as well as Aaron: and God promised to speak to him in that little room.*

I am glad, my dear children, that there is a brighter place where we may go one day, and hear God speak to us.

God desired Moses to have some beautiful clothes made for Aaron to wear. The two clever men, of whom I told you before, knew how to make them.

* There will I meet with thee, and I will commune with thee from above the mercy-seat.—Ex. xxv. 22. Also Numb. vii. 89.

These were the clothes Aaron was to wear.

1. He was to wear a white dress with long sleeves.

2. A robe of blue. He was to wear this over the white dress. Little golden bells were hung round the edge of it: and they would sound sweetly as Aaron moved along.

3. An ephod made of white linen, worked all over with purple, scarlet, and gold. Aaron was to wear the ephod over the blue robe.

4. A band round his waist called a girdle. It was made of white linen, and was worked with purple, scarlet thread, and with gold wire.

5. A breastplate. Aaron was to wear this in front. It was made of linen, covered with twelve shining stones. It was to be fastened to Aaron's shoulders by gold chains.

6. A mitre. Aaron was to wear a high white cap upon his head, called a mitre. A piece of gold was on the mitre, and on the gold was written, "Holiness to the Lord." Aaron ought to be holy because he was to offer sacrifices to God.

Aaron was to wear no shoes upon his feet: but he was often to wash his feet and his hands in the brass basin.

Aaron had four sons. God said that they should help him to offer sacrifices. Aaron's sons were to wear white clothes, but not the same beautiful clothes as Aaron. They were to be called "Priests," and Aaron was to be called "High Priest."

It was a long while before the tabernacle was made. Though all the people worked very hard, yet the things were not finished for almost a year.

At last God desired Moses to set up the tabernacle.

Moses set up the boards for the walls of the tabernacle, and covered the top with curtains: and he placed the ark in the Holy of Holies: and he put the table, and the candlestick, and the golden altar, in the largest room: and he set up the posts, and the curtains, all round the court: and he put the brass altar and basin in it. Then Moses poured sweet oil upon all the things: this pouring oil was called "anointing."

Then Moses put upon Aaron his beautiful clothes, and put the white clothes upon Aaron's sons: and he poured sweet oil upon their heads, and anointed them.

Then God came down in his cloud, and his brightness filled the whole place: and so God showed that he would have it for his house.

Was it not pleasant for the Israelites to think that God lived in a house in the midst of them? The cloud could be seen outside the tabernacle as well as inside: and in the night it shone like fire. How kind it was in God to let the people see some of his brightness! God wished them to be very good, and to obey all he said. God is very near us, too, though we cannot see him; but we hope to see him some day.

What place is much more beautiful than the tabernacle was? Heaven. If we get to heaven, we shall be much more glorious than Aaron was, and we shall see God's face for ever and ever, and so we shall be quite happy.

THE HIGH PRIEST'S DRESS.

1. The white coat, with long sleeves.
2. The blue robe.
3. The ephod.
4. The girdle.
5. The breast-plate.
6. The mitre.

How fair was Aaron to the view,
  When in his splendid garments drest,
He wore his robe of heavenly blue
  Above his long and snowy vest.

His ephod and his girdle white
  Were wrought with purple, gold, and red:
Upon his breast shone jewels bright,
  A costly mitre on his head.

No priest like him dwells now on earth,
  But there is one beyond the sky;
Ah! who can set his glories forth,
  Or who with him in beauty vie?

O fairer than the sons of men,*
  O fairest of the hosts above,†
What tongue can tell, what eye hath seen,
  The glories of the God of love?

* Thou art fairer than the children of men.—Ps. xlv. 2

† Who in the heaven can be compared unto the Lord?—Ps. lxxxix. 6.

O! may I thy sweet image wear,
When from the tomb my flesh shall rise,
And on the fairest of the fair
Forever fix my loving eyes!

CHAPTER XXXI.

MOSES, OR THE JOURNEY OF THE ISRAELITES.

Now the Israelites had a place in which to worship God, and to offer sacrifices.

Every morning the priests offered up a lamb on the brass altar,* and burned incense on the golden altar in the tabernacle.† And every evening they offered another lamb, and burned some more incense.

God sent some fire down from heaven to burn the sacrifices with,‡ and the priests never let the fire go out; and the priests always kept the lamps burning in the tabernacle. Every sabbath-day the priests placed some fresh bread on the golden table; and when they put the fresh bread on it, they took away the old bread, and ate it themselves.§

The people went into the great court of the tabernacle to worship God, and to see the lamb killed and burned on the altar. Afterwards they saw Aaron go into the tabernacle to burn incense. The people stood in the court while Aaron was in the

* Exodus xxix. 38—41.
† Exodus xxx. 7, 8.
‡ Leviticus ix. 24.
§ Leviticus xxiv. 5—9.

tabernacle praying for them. They waited till he came out again to bless them. He lifted up his hands and said, "The Lord bless thee, and keep thee."*

Who prays for us in heaven? Who will come one day, and bless us?

The Lord Jesus Christ. He is our High Priest.

While the people had been making the tabernacle, they had stayed in one place near the great mount, Sinai; but soon after it was finished, the cloud of God moved. Then the priests blew two silver trumpets.

Why did they blow these trumpets?

To tell the people that they were to move to another place.

Then the people packed up their tents and furniture, and put them on the backs of their camels and asses.

Then the priests went into the tabernacle, and covered all the things in it with blue cloth. No one might look while they were covering the things. Then they gave them to some men to carry upon their shoulders:† but the priests covered the ark with the beautiful veil, and they carried it themselves.‡ There were two long golden sticks fastened to it, the priests held the ends of the sticks, and so they carried it.

Then the priests desired some men to carry the curtains, and the posts, and the boards of the taber-

* Numbers vi. 23. to end. † Luke i. 9, 10, 22. Numbers iv. 5—15.
‡ The priests (the sons of Levi) which bare the ark.—Deut xxxi. 9

nacle.* The priests went first † with tne ark, and all the people followed them, and God in the cloud showed them the way.

When the cloud stopped, the priests and the people stopped, and set up the tabernacle and the tents.‡

In this manner the Israelites travelled all through the wilderness.

What a happy people they were, to have such a God to show them the way to Canaan! They ought always to have been praising Him for his goodness. He fed them with manna, and gave them water from the rock; and he had promised to bring them to a sweet land. Besides all this, he had promised to send his Son to die for them; and the lambs were killed, you know, to make them remember that promise.

I hope we shall not forget how Jesus died upon the cross. And I hope we shall get to that sweet land, called heaven. God wishes us to get there, and Jesus Christ is praying for us.

While Israel in the desert stray,
  They feel God's tender care;—
For heavenly blessings day by day
  Are shed upon them there.

At earliest dawn they gather bread,
  New fallen from the skies;
And next the holy courts they tread,
  And view the sacrifice.

* Numbers v. 23—33. † Numbers x. 33. ‡ Numbers ix. 15 to end

It is for *them* the spotless lamb
  Is to the altar led!
It is for *them* the purple stream
  Is on the altar shed.

And Aaron lifts for *them* a prayer,
  As he the incense burns;
Filling with odours sweet the air,
  To bless them he returns.

Those days are past: Aaron no more
  For Israel intercedes;
The skies no more sweet manna pour,
  The lamb no longer bleeds.

But *we* partake of heavenly bread,
  In God's sweet word of grace:
For us the heavenly Lamb has bled;
  For us a Saviour prays.

O that we may more grateful be
  Than Israel was of old,
And sweeter days we yet shall see
  Within God's heavenly fold.

CHAPTER XXXII.

MOSES, OR THE TWELVE SPIES.

Numbers xiii.: xiv. 1—40.

At last the Israelites came quite near the land of Canaan.

They could see the tops of the high hills that were in Canaan, and they wished to know what sort of a land it was, and what sort of people lived in it.

So the Israelites came to Moses and said, "We wish to send some men to look at the land, and we wish them to come back and tell us what kind of a land it is."*

Would Moses send some men?

Moses waited to know whether God would like some men to go.

Soon God said to Moses, "Send twelve men into Canaan to see the land." So Moses called twelve of the children of Israel, and said to them, "Go into Canaan, and walk up among the high mountains, and look at the land: see whether there are many people living in the land, and what kind of people they are; whether they are strong or weak: see whether there are many trees, and much corn and grass in the land; and bring back some fruit, to show us the kind of fruit that grows in the land."

So the twelve men set out on their journey. These men were called the twelve spies. They walked up and down the hills, and by the side of the water. They saw sweet gardens, and some fields covered with sheep, and some fields full of corn, and trees laden with fruit, and they saw holes in the trees, which the bees had filled with honey, so that honey dropped to the ground. They saw large towns with high walls around them, and they saw many strong men and some of them were giants.

At last they came to a brook or pond. A vine

* Deut. i. 22.

grew by it, and on the vine there were ripe grapes—one of the bunches was very, very large. They said, "Let us bring it back, to show to the children of Israel." One man could not carry this bunch by himself. So they took a staff or stick, and fastened the bunch of grapes to the staff, and one man held one end of the staff and another held the other. The rest of the men picked figs and other fruit and carried them back to the tents.

The spies were forty days looking at the land of Canaan.

When they came back, the people saw the beautiful bunch of grapes. There were no such grapes in the wilderness. The spies then said, "The land of Canaan is a fine land, full of milk and honey: but we cannot get into it, for the people live in great towns with high walls: they are very strong, and some of them are giants, and when we saw them, we felt as if we were as little as grasshoppers."

Then the children of Israel were very much frightened, and they began to murmur and to weep.

"Ah!" said the people, "we shall be killed if we try to get in."

It was wicked to say this, because God had promised to help the Israelites to get into Canaan. It is wicked not to believe what God says.

Two of the spies were very good men; their names were Joshua and Caleb. They did not wish to frighten the people; and Caleb stood up and said, " Let us go into the land, for we can conquer the people that are in it."

But the ten other spies said, " No, we cannot, because the people of Canaan are stronger than we."

These ten spies were very wicked men, because they knew that God had promised to help the Israelites to conquer the men of Canaan, and they ought to have told the people to trust in God.

The Israelites cried all night long, and they were angry with Moses and Aaron for bringing them out of Egypt, and said, " O that we had died in Egypt, or in the wilderness! The people of Canaan will kill us with their swords, and they will kill our wives and our little children."

They spoke in this way all night long, instead of praying to God to help them.

At last they said, " Let us go back into Egypt."

They knew that Moses would not take them back. So they said, " We can make another man captain over us, and he will take us back to Egypt."

Moses and Aaron heard these wicked words: they were full of grief, and they fell down on the ground upon their faces.

What had grieved Moses and Aaron?

They were grieved to see the people so wicked.

Then Joshua and Caleb stood up and said to the people, " we have seen the land, and it is a very beautiful land; and if we trust in God, he will help us to fight; but the people of Canaan have no God to help them; therefore we ought not to be afraid of them."

The children of Israel would not listen to Joshua and Caleb, but were going to kill them with stones, when God shone brightly upon the tabernacle, so that the people saw that he was angry.

Moses was lying on his face on the ground, but God spoke to him, and said, "How long will this people provoke me? I will kill them with a plague."

Then Moses prayed to God for the people.

"O pardon this people," he said, "their great sin. Thou hast forgiven them many times, and thy mercy is very great."

God heard Moses' prayer, and said, "I have pardoned them. I will not kill them all now, but they shall not come into Canaan;—only their children shall come in. They shall stay in the wilderness forty years, and they shall all die in it; and when their children are grown up, they shall go into the land of Canaan. But there are two of the men who shall go into Canaan,—they are Caleb and Joshua."

Moses told the children of Israel what God had said, and when the people heard it, they were very unhappy, and they murmured.

The ten wicked spies soon fell sick and died, but Joshua and Caleb lived still.

How sad it was for the people to think that they should never see that sweet land of Canaan, but should die in the wilderness! Yet they deserved to die, because they had not believed what God had said.

God has promised to give us his Spirit if we ask him, and to take us to heaven. Do you believe this promise, dear children? Then you will ask God for his Spirit. But if you do not care about heaven, then you will not pray to God for his Spirit. Then God will be angry, and at last he will say that you shall never get to heaven.*

"Is that fair Canaan's coast?
Are those her mountains high?"
Cry Israel's eager host,
As in the camp they lie.
"Let's send a little band
Of brave and faithful men,
To search the pleasant land,
And bring us word again."
The chosen band departs:
What scenes before them rise,
To charm their anxious hearts,
And their astonished eyes!

They climb the mountain's side,
Whence cooling waters flow:
They cross the valleys wide,
Where golden harvests grow;
Pass through the woods, where bees
Sip honey from each flower,†
And in the hollow trees
Hide their delicious store;

* Let us therefore labour to enter into that rest, lest any man fall after the same example of unbelief.—Heb. iv. 11.

† All they of the land came to a wood, and there was honey upon the ground.—Samuel xiv. 25.

View gardens where the vine
  And olive tree are seen,
The sheep and lowing kine
  Amidst the pastures green.

But while the beauteous land
  They view with great delight,
They see where cities stand
  With walls of wondrous height,
And towers tall and strong,
  And gates of iron and brass:
And 'midst the countless throng,
  Some who the rest surpass:
Men of enormous size,
  Who wield the sword and spear,
And in whose sight the spies
  Like grasshoppers appear.

But why should such a sight
  Fill Israel with dismay?
Their God for them shall fight,
  And they shall win the day:—
For idols are adored
  By Canaan's wicked race,
And cups of blood are poured
  Before each idol's face,*
And helpless babies bleed
  Amongst the thickest trees,
And every wicked deed
  Is done, those gods to please,†

CHILD.

There is a land more fair
  Than any land below,

Their drink offerings of blood will I not offer.—Psalm xvi. 4.
† Every abomination to the Lord, which he hateth, have they done unto their gods.—Leviticus xii. 31.

And I would enter there,
  In spite of every foe.
Then let me now begin
  To strive with all my might
To overcome all sin,*
  However hard the fight.
The Lord will give me strength,
  And fill my soul with grace,
And I shall reach at length
  His heavenly dwelling-place.

CHAPTER XXXIII.

MOSES, OR THE SIN OF MOSES AND AARON.

Numbers xx. 1—13, 22—29.

THE children of Israel lived in the wilderness a great many years. They moved about from place to place.

At last they came to a place where there was no water.

How do you think they behaved? Did they pray to God, or did they murmur?

They murmured against Moses and Aaron, as they always did when they were unhappy.

They said, "O that we had died before this time! Why did you bring us out of Egyyt into this wilderness? Here there are no figs, no grapes,

* If ye, through the Spirit, do mortify the deeds of the body, ye shall live.—Romans viii. 13.

no kind of nice fruit, and now there is no water to drink."

They forgot that it was because of their own wickedness that they were still in the wilderness; for if they had obeyed God, they would then have been sitting under their own trees, eating their own fruit in Canaan.

Moses and Aaron were very much grieved to near them murmur, and they went away from the people, and fell on their faces before the tabernacle; and soon God spoke to them.

He said "Take the rod and call the people, and go to the rock and speak to it, and water shall come out of the rock, and then the people and the beasts shall drink."

So Moses took the rod, (the rod was kept near the ark.) Then Moses and Aaron called the people together, and told them to look at what they were going to do.

Moses and Aaron felt very angry with the people, and they said, "Hear now, ye rebels! (which means *grumblers*,) must we fetch water for you out of this rock?"

Then Moses lifted up his hand and struck the rock twice with his rod; and the water came flowing out in streams, and the people and the cattle began to drink.

Do you think that Moses and Aaron had behaved right? Had God told them to strike the rock?

God had said, "speak to the rock."

Was it right to speak so impatiently, and to say, "Must we fetch water for you, rebels?"

Moses and Aaron had been in a passion. God was displeased with them.

Do you think that God will punish them? God loved Moses and Aaron; yet he would punish them when they did wrong. He would forgive them and take them to heaven, but he would give them some punishment.* You shall hear what the punishment should be.

Soon afterwards, God said to Moses and Aaron, "Because you have done this, you shall not go into Canaan; you shall die in the wilderness."

What a great punishment this was! Moses had often longed to see that sweet land of Canaan; he had often wished to see the Israelites happy in their own houses and gardens; he had longed to see the place where Abraham had built altars and worshipped God; but now he must die in the wilderness. He prayed to God to excuse him this punishment, but God would not. God said "Ask me no more to do this." Then Moses knew that he must bear this punishment.†

Moses was the meekest man in all the world. The Israelites had often spoken ungratefully to him, and he had made no answer. Yet at last he himself fell into a passion.

You see how much God hates passion. God

* Thou wast a God that forgavest them, though thou tookest vengeance of their inventions.—Psalm xcix. 8.

† Deuteronomy iii. 23—26.

wishes us to be very meek, like the Lord Jesus Christ, who never spoke an angry word.

Are you meek, my dear child? Can you bear to be pushed, and slapped, and not push and slap again? If a child takes your place, can you ask him gently to let you have it; and if he will not, can you take another quietly? When children call you rude names, can you be gentle, and not call them rude names too? A meek child can do all these things. God can make you very meek, my dear child. Will you pray to God to make you meek, like Jesus? Moses, too, was very meek, though he fell into a passion once.

Was it unkind in God to punish Moses and Aaron?

God cannot be unkind, but he will punish people for disobedience. God wished to show the Israelites that he would not allow any person to be disobedient, not even Moses.

At last the time came for Aaron to die: for God chose Aaron to die first. God said to Moses, "Go up to the top of the hill with Aaron, and take Aaron's eldest son with you; and Aaron will die on the top, and you must put his clothes upon his son." God chose Aaron's son to be high priest instead of Aaron, so he was to wear Aaron's clothes.

So Aaron put on his beautiful high priest's clothes; his blue robe with golden bells, and his shining ephod over it, his shining breastplate, and his white mitre, with the golden writing upon it. Then Aaron walked with Moses and his son to the top of the hill, and all the people looked at them as they were walking up. Aaron knew that he should never walk down that hill, but still he obeyed God, and bore his punishment meekly.

When they were come to the top, Moses took the beautiful clothes off his brother Aaron, and put them upon Aaron's son.

Moses parted from his brother Aaron on the top of that hill: for there Aaron died. Moses and the son left him dead upon the top, and came down the hill together. Then the people saw that Aaron was dead, and that there was another high priest.

Aaron's soul went up to heaven, for God had forgiven him. If he had not spoken so angrily, he would have lived to see the land of Canaan. Moses knew that he should die very soon: but God did not choose him to die yet.

The mountain steep see Aaron climb,
  While *two* alone his journey share.
How bright his splendid garments shine!
  What charming fragrance fills the air!

How sweetly sounds each golden bell,
  Oft heard within the holy place!
Listen! It is the priest's farewell:—
  Israel no more shall see his face.

The aged priest shall ne'er return,
  Ne'er lift his holy hands to bless,
Nor trim the lamp nor incense burn,
  Nor Israel's sins with blood confess.

Upon the mountain's height he stands:
  And Moses now, with pious care,

Loosens the breastplate's golden bands,
  And strips him of his garments fair.

Then Aaron yields the breath he drew,
  And sleeps upon that mountain's brow;
His girdle bright, and robe of blue,
  Adorn young Eleazer now.

It is for sin that Aaron dies;
  O had he still obeyed his God,
Nor let his hasty passion rise,
  Sweet Canaan's fields he should have trod.

But though a *sinful* priest must die,
  That none may on his prayers depend:
Our *sinless* Priest still lives on high,
  And *his* fair days shall never end.

His glorious robes he *ever* wears,
  Still lifts his holy hands to bless;
Like incense sweet presents our prayers,
  Perfum'd in his own righteousness.

CHAPTER XXXIV.

MOSES, OR THE SERPENT OF BRASS.

Numbers xxi. 4—9.

The children of Israel travelled in the wilderness a great many years. Sometimes when they were close to Canaan, the cloud moved the other way and the Israelites were obliged to go on travelling in the wilderness. This made them very unhappy, for they longed very much to get into the sweet land of Canaan. If they had not behaved so ill in the wilderness, they would soon have got to Canaan: but God punished them by not letting them get in.

How do you think they bore their punishment? You know that they were always ready to murmur. They spoke against God and against Moses. They said, "Why have you brought us out of Egypt? We shall die in the wilderness. There is no bread, nor any water here, and we do not like this manna."

Was the manna nice food? It was fit for angels, spotless, white, and sweet as honey; it came down from heaven and did not grow out of the ground, as corn does. Yet these ungrateful Israelites said that they hated it, and were tired of eating it.

God sent them a dreadful punishment this time. You know that there were wild beasts and horrible serpents and scorpions in the wilderness; but God took care of the Israelites, so that they were not hurt by them; but now God sent serpents, whose mouths burned like fire. These serpents came rushing among the tents. The Israelites could not get away from them. If the Israelites climbed up a high place, the serpents could climb after them and they could get through the smallest places.

Many, many of the Israelites were bitten by these serpents. After they had been bitten they grew sick, and were full of pain, and got worse and worse, till at last they died. There was no medicine could cure these bites; no plaster would make them well; every person who was bitten was sure to die.

The Israelites came to Moses, and said, "We have sinned: we have spoken against the Lord, and against you; pray to the Lord that he take the serpents from us." For the serpents were still among the tents.

Did Moses pray to God for the people? or did he say, "You deserved to be punished, and I will not help you?" Moses was kind and forgiving, and he prayed for the people.

The Lord heard Moses' prayer, and he did more than Moses asked, for God not only called away the serpents, but he told him how to cure the people who were bitten by the serpents.

What do you think God told Moses to do? Did he tell Moses to give them some medicine, or to put a plaster to the bites? You will be surprised to hear the strange things that God told Moses to do.

He said, "Take some brass, and make it into the image of a serpent, and put it on a pole, and tell the people who are bitten to look at it, and those who look shall be made well."

Was not this a strange way of making them well?

Moses believed God. He took some brass, and made it soft in the fire; and then made it like one of the fiery serpents, and put it on a pole, and lifted it up, where every one could see it, and called to the sick people to look quickly at the serpent, and be made well.

The people who were bitten could crawl to the door of their tents, and lift up their dying eyes towards the serpent. After they had looked, their pain went away; they felt well and strong: they could walk and praise God.

Did all the people who were sick look at the serpent? I do not know. Perhaps some said, "How should looking at a serpent make us well?" If there were any such people, they must have died. But I hope that all looked at the serpent.

And now dear children, do you know that a serpent has bitten us? A serpent has bitten our souls. What serpent do I mean? The old serpent, the devil. He has bitten our souls; that is, he has made us naughty. You have heard how he made Adam and Eve naughty in the garden of Eden. We are naughty too, because we are Adam's children. Who can make our souls well of this bite? Who can make us good? If we are not made good, our souls will die; they will go to hell. Jesus can make us good by sending his Spirit into our hearts.

The serpent of brass was lifted on a pole,—Jesus was lifted up on the cross:—now we must look at Jesus. What do I mean by looking at Jesus? I do not mean looking at him with our eyes: it would not make us good to see Jesus on the cross. A great many wicked people saw him die, and were not made good. The "looking" I mean is thinking of him, and loving him. When you think of Jesus having died for you, and when you love him for it, then you look at him with your soul.

I hope, dear children, that you will all think of Jesus, and that God will send his Holy Spirit into your hearts, and make you good, and let you live forever in heaven.

Hear a poor Israelite complain,
  "Oh, can no med'cine then be found
To ease my agonising pain;
  No balm to heal my festering wound!"

This earth no med'cine can supply,
  No balm to heal the serpent's bite:
But lift once more thy dying eye,
  And thou shalt live, poor Israelite.

He looks on high, and sees a pole,
  Round which a brazen serpent coils;
No more his eyes with anguish roll,
  No more his blood with fever boils.

Nor does the sight heal one alone:
  A thousand dying sufferers gaze,
And every shriek, and every groan,
  Are turn'd to joyful songs of praise.

CHILD.

This history seems to me a glass,
  In which I can my Saviour see,
As Moses rear'd that form of brass,
  So Christ was lifted on the tree.

Full well I know the reason why
  Upon that tree my Saviour hung;
He saw us at the point to die,
  Wounded by Satan's lying tongue.

He saw the serpent's poisonous fangs
  Make pride to swell, and rage to burn,
Fill us with envy's gnawing pangs,
  And spotless hearts to devils turn.

He saw—he pitied—and he bore
  Our sins upon the bloody tree;
He bade us *look*, that evermore
  From sin and death we might be free.

O Lord! 'tis not with *fleshly* eyes
  That I am bid on thee to gaze;
My *inward* eyes can pierce the skies,
  Those inward eyes to thee I raise.

If on thy death I meditate,
  And pardon for thy sake entreat,
My soul's disease will soon abate,
  And groans be changed to praises sweet.

CHAPTER XXXV.

MOSES, OR THE DEATH OF MOSES.

Deut. xxxi. xxxii. xxxiii. xxxiv.

THE time was almost come for Moses to die. The Israelites were very soon to go into Canaan, but Moses was not to go there with them.

Moses had written a great many books while he had been in the wilderness: and now he had almost finished them. Should you like to know what Moses had written about in these books?

He had written about how God made the world, how Adam ate the fruit, how Cain killed Abel. He had written about Noah, and Abraham, and Isaac, and Jacob; he had written about sweet Joseph and his wicked brethren: he had written about himself, how he had been saved from the water when he was a baby. He had written about the ten plagues, and the ten commandments, and the tabernacle; he had written about his own sin. All I have told you Moses had written down in five books; they have all been copied in other books, and we can read all Moses wrote, for it is in the Bible.

But how did Moses know all these things? He was not born when God made the world. How could he write about things he never saw? Could anybody have told him how God made the world? No one was born when God made the world: no one but God could tell him, and God did tell him.

God spake to Moses by his Spirit: while Moses was writing with his pen, God was putting thoughts in his mind; so he always knew what to write.

Moses did not write in such books as you have seen. His paper was rolled up like a piece of cloth in the shop. He wrote five rolls; and these he called his books. If you had read in Moses' book, you must have unrolled it as you read it.

When Moses had done writing his books, he called the priests, and told them to take care of his books. Moses said to them, "You must read these books to all the Israelites, to the men, the women, and the little children, that they may know how to please God."

Moses knew that he must soon leave the Israelites. He wished very much that some good man should take care of them after he was dead; for he loved them very much, though they had behaved so ill to him. So Moses begged God to give them to the care of some good man;* and God heard his prayer, and said to Moses, "I have found a man, who will take care of the children of Israel after you are dead."

Who do you think this man was? It was Joshua, one of the good spies; he had helped Moses to do God's work for forty years;† so that Moses had taught him a great deal. Moses was very glad that Joshua would take care of the Israelites when he was dead.

Moses called Joshua, and said to him, "God will let you take the children of Israel into Canaan: you must be very brave, for you will have to fight against the wicked people; but God will help you: so do not be afraid. God will never leave you, nor forsake you.

Moses wished to speak to the people before he died, and advise them to be good; so Moses called all the people together, and told them he was going to die. "I am very old," said he; "I am

* And Moses spake unto the Lord, saying, "Let the Lord, the God of the spirit of all flesh, set a man over the congregation," &c. Numbers xxvii. 15, 16.

† Joshua was Moses' Minister, when God spake from Mount Sinai, forty years before his death. Ex. xxiv. 13.

a hundred and twenty years old this day. I offended *God*, and I must not go into the land of Canaan; but Joshua will take you there. Remember to obey God, and to love him, and he will always bless you: but if you worship idols, and are wicked, God will punish you."

God told Moses to teach the people a song, that they might sing it after he was dead. This song was about God's kindness to the children of Israel.

My dear children, you learn pretty songs or hymns about God. Do you know why you are taught to repeat them? It is to help you to think of God, that you may love him. Some children repeat their hymns as soon as they awake in the morning.

After Moses had taught the people the song, he blessed them, and then he left them for ever.

God said to Moses, "Go up that high mountain alone. I cannot let you go into Canaan, but I will let you see the beautiful land of Canaan from the top of that mountain."

Moses was glad that he might see Canaan, though he might not go in. So Moses went up the mountain quite alone. He was very old, yet he was not weak; he could walk as well as when he was young, and he could see as well; for his eyes were not dim;—he read, and wrote, and saw things far off. God had not let him grow weak or blind.

I think the Israelites must have felt very sad when they saw Moses go up that mountain all alone, and when they knew they should see him no more.

I hope they felt sorry for having behaved so ill to him, and for having so provoked him at the rock. What a kind friend Moses had been to them!

When Moses was at the top of the hill, he looked and saw the land of Canaan a great way off. It was a beautiful land, and full of green hills, and rivers, of fields ripe with corn, and of trees laden with fruit. Moses was glad that the children of Israel would live in such a sweet land, where they might worship God.

When Moses had looked at the land, he died. No friend was near to close his eyes, or to hear his last sigh: no brother's hand was there to wrap him in his grave-clothes, or to cover him with the green earth.

Would God leave Moses' body to be eaten by the wild beasts, to be picked by the birds of the air? No; God himself buried Moses, not upon the top of the hill but in some secret place under the hill. No one knows where Moses lies, but the angels, who carried his soul to God: they know, for they watch over God's dear children in the dust. When the last trumpet sounds, Moses will rise from that grave, and shine like the stars in the sky.

Thus Moses died. He was the only man to whom God talked as to a friend: God spoke to Moses face to face, as friends talk to each other.

I shall tell you no more of Moses; but you will see him in heaven if you go there. You remember that he might have been a prince in the land of Egypt. King Pharaoh's daughter saved him from the water, and she gave him fine things, and called him her son. But Moses wished to help the poor children of Israel, and he did not choose to be a prince in Egypt.

Was *it* not much better that Moses should help the poor children of Israel, than that he should be rich and grand?

You see that God loved Moses, and made him his friend, and took him to heaven when he died.

Now my dear children I hope you will be like Moses. I hope that when you are grown up, you will not try to get fine things, but that you will try to help poor people, and teach them about God. Think, dear children, how kind Jesus has been to you. He left heaven that he might save us, and that we might know God.

"O beauteous land! of cooling streams,
And mountains crowned with flowers;
How oft have I, in pleasant dreams,
Worshipp'd within thy bowers!

"I love the land where Abraham rear'd
The altars to his God;
And where the Lord has oft appear'd,
Where angels' feet have trod;

"I see from far a joyful morn
Dawn on that land of rest;

For there a Saviour shall be born,
  To make all nations blest.*

"Though now I die at God's command,
  This hope sustains my heart;
And to a fairer, purer land
  I joyfully depart."

What though no earthly friend was near,
  To close the prophet's eyes;
No children laid him in his bier,
  With loving tears and sighs.—

A heavenly train his soul convey'd
  To mansions of the blest,
His precious body gently laid
  Where none should break his rest.

No eye has seen the grassy bed,
  Where now the prophet lies;
But when the trump shall wake the dead,
  How glorious shall he rise!

CHAPTER XXXVI.

JOSHUA, OR RAHAB.

Joshua ii.

THE Israelites were now come close to the land of Canaan. They were sorry that Moses was dead; but Joshua was now to take care of them instead of Moses. Joshua was to tell them what

* Had ye believed Moses, ye would have believed me, for he wrote of me.—John v. 46.

to do. God would speak to Joshua, and Joshua would tell them what God said.

The Israelites would soon have to fight a great deal. Whom would they have to fight against? The wicked people who lived in Canaan. God chose that they should be killed to punish them for their wickedness, and God chose that the Israelites should live in their land instead of them.

There was a great river that rolled between the wilderness and Canaan. The Israelites would be obliged to cross the river before they could get into Canaan. The Israelites could see the green hills of Canaan on the other side of the river, and they saw a great town also, with high walls all round it. This town was called Jericho. It was in Canaan, and wicked people lived in it. The Israelites knew that they would soon have to fight against the people who lived in this town.

Joshua told two of the Israelites to go to the town, and to look at it, and to come back, and tell him about the town, and about the people who lived in it. These men were called 'spies,' because they were sent to spy, or to look at the town.

Joshua did not wish the people of Jericho to know when these two spies came into the town, lest the wicked people should kill them. So they went to the town when it was almost dark. The spies got over the river: there was one place in the river where the water was not very deep, and where people could get over. This was called a ford.

The gate of Jericho used to be shut when it was dark; but the spies came just before the gate was shut. They went to the house of a woman named Rahab, who kept an inn. Her house was built upon the wall of Jericho. The spies hoped that nobody had seen them come into Jericho; but some people had seen them, and these people went and told the king of Jericho that two Israelites were in Rahab's house. The king of Jericho knew that the Israelites meant to come and fight against him; so he wanted to kill these two spies, and he sent some men to Rahab's house to bring them to him.

What could the poor spies do? where could they go? But God took care of them. He put it into Rahab's heart to be kind to them. Rahab had taken the spies, when they first came, to the top of her house to hide them. The roof of her house was not slanting like the roof of this house; it was flat like the floor. On the roof of Rahab's house there were a great many stalks of flax. What is flax? Flax is a plant; and the stalks of flax are made into thread. Rahab had spread these stalks upon the roof of her house to dry them. When the spies had climbed up the stairs to the top of the house, she told them to lie down; and she covered them all over with the stalks, so that nobody could see them.

The men who were come to bring the spies to the king of Jericho, could not find them in Rahab's house; so they went to look for them outside the city, among the hills, and by the river-side.

When the king of Jericho's men were gone, Rahab crept up the stairs to speak to the spies. It was night, so she could talk to them on the roof without being seen. The men came from under the heaps of flax. Rahab had been taught to worship idols; but you will see that she now believed in the true God, and not in idols. She had a great favour to ask of the spies. She was very much afraid lest, when the Israelites should come over the river to fight against Jericho, they should kill her and her friends; so now she begged the spies to promise to save her, and those she loved.

Poor Rahab said, "I know that God will let the people of Israel come and live in Canaan. Everybody is very much frightened lest you should kill them. We have heard how your God helped you to pass through the Red Sea. I know that your God is the only true God. Now promise that when you come to this town, you will not kill me, and my father, and mother, and brothers, and sisters. I have been kind to you, and will you be kind to me?"

Do you think that the spies would promise to save Rahab and her friends? O yes! How kind she had been to them in hiding them! Besides this, Rahab feared God. The spies promised that they would not let her be killed, or her father, or mother, or brothers, or sisters.

How glad Rahab must have been when they

made her this promise! There was one thing the spies desired her not to do; that was, not to tell anybody about their having been to Jericho. The spies said, "If you will not tell anybody about our having come here, we promise to save your life, and the life of your father, and mother, and brothers, and sisters."

Then Rahab helped the spies to get out of the town. Could the spies go out at the gates? It was night, and the gates were shut. If the spies waited till the morning, the people of Jericho would see them going out, and would kill them. But Rahab found a way of letting the spies go.

Her house was built on the wall of Jericho, one of the windows in her house looked towards the green hills outside of Jericho. This window was high; so Rahab took a rope, and tied the rope round one of the men, and let him down from the window; and then she tied the rope round the other man, and let him down.

When the men were standing on the ground outside the wall of Jericho, they called to Rahab, who was looking out of the window, and they said, "Take that red rope, and bind it to your window; bring your father, and mother, and brothers, and sisters, into your house. If they stay in it with you, we promise that they shall not be killed when the Israelites come to fight against this town; but if you or any of your relations are walking in the streets when we come, then, perhaps, you or they may be killed. Neither may you tell any other person about our having come here: you must keep it a secret." When the spies had said this, they went away, and they hid themselves among the hills for three days, lest the men of Jericho should be watching by the river to kill them. At the end of three days they got over the river, and came back to Joshua, and told him all that had happened. Joshua was glad to hear that the people of Jericho were so much frightened, and he felt sure that God would help him to conquer all the people in Canaan.

The spies told Joshua about Rahab. They said, "You will know which house is Rahab's, because she has bound a red rope to the window." Joshua desired that nobody would kill the people in the house with the red rope on the window.

Do you think that Rahab forgot to bind the red rope on her window? O no! she bound it there, and she brought her father, and mother, and brothers, and sisters, into her house; and she did not tell any of the wicked people of Jericho about the spies. Nobody knew why she bound a red rope to her window.

Do you think that Rahab felt frightened now? Could she not trust the spies? Would they break their word? How Rahab must have thanked God for promising to save her, when the people of Jericho would be killed!

My dear children, is there a day coming when a great many wicked people will be killed and burned in the fire? You have heard of the judgment day. Do you not hope that God will save you in that day? Then do as Rahab did. Ask God to promise to save you. He will save you if you ask him. If you are really afraid of God, as Rahab was, you will not do wicked things to make him angry; but you will often pray to him to make you good and to forgive you for Jesus Christ's sake.

God will hear you, and he will remember his promise in the judgment-day, and he will not let you be hurt.

With softest step and troubled air,
In silence Rahab climbs the stair
Screen'd by darkness of the skies
Upon the roof, with Israel's spies,
She trembling stands; before them falls,
And earnestly for mercy calls.

"O people, whom the Lord has led,
Your deeds have fill'd the earth with dread;
We've heard how once you crossed the sea,
And how you made two nations flee.
What pangs of terror then we felt!
How did the hearts of warriors melt!

Against your God what can we do?
The only God, the great, the true—
Your armies soon will tread this shore,
O now for mercy I implore!"

Thus Rahab pours her humble prayer;
Nor do the spies refuse to swear
Their kind deliverer's life to spare.

How gratefully poor Rahab hastes
To bind a cord around their waists;

The spies observe its scarlet hue,
And choose it for their token true;
Gently to earth they both descend,
Then cry, "Let Rahab now attend;
This cord unto your window bind,
So you and those you love shall find
Beneath that roof a safe retreat,
When all besides destruction meet."

How gladly Rahab binds the thread
Which shall from danger shield her head!
How quickly bids her kindred come,
And find a refuge in her home!

CHILD.

Is there no thread that I may bind,
And in the judgment mercy find?
Ah! yes, the blood that Jesus shed,
Was imag'd by that scarlet thread,
O! may this blood my soul adorn,
In the tremendous judgment morn.

Let none mistake me while I sing:
I speak not of an *earthly* thing;
This blood is sprinkled upon all
Who on their dying Saviour call;
By angels shall the mark be seen;
That sign from death their souls shall screen *

And I would join in Rahab's prayer,
And cry, "O God, my kindred spare!
My father, who protects my youth,
O let him know, thy power and truth;

* Let us draw near with a true heart, in full assurance of faith, having our hearts *sprinkled* from an evil conscience.
Elect . . . . . . unto obedience, and sprinkling of the blood of Jesus Christ.—1 Peter i. 2
And he shall send his angels with a great sound of a trumpet, and they shall gather together his elect from the four winds.—Matt. xxiv. 31

And her who nursed my infancy,
And those who share her love with me,
Within some secret chamber hide,
When thousands fall on every side."*

CHAPTER XXXVII.

JOSHUA, OR THE RIVER JORDAN.

Joshua iii. iv. v. 1, 11, 12.

THE people of Israel were now close to Canaan; but a deep river ran between the wilderness and Canaan. It was called the river Jordan. How were the Israelites to get over it?

Could they go over in boats?

How could wood be got to make boats for so many people?

Could they make a bridge? The people in Canaan would have shot arrows at the Israelites while they were making a bridge.

Could they swim over?

How could the children and the women swim? and how could they take their tents over?

God could help them to get over. How had they got over the Red Sea?

You shall hear what God told Joshua to do.

Joshua rose up early in the morning, and he said

* Come, my people, enter thou into thy chambers; hide thyself as it were, for a little moment, until the indignation be overpast. Isaiah xxvi. 20.

to the people, "Look and see where the priests take the ark, and do you follow them, but do not go too near."

Then Joshua said to the priests, "Take up the ark, and walk on."

The ark (which was a golden box) was covered with a blue cloth, that none might see it, or see the golden angels on the top. Two long sticks were run through little rings joined in the ark, and the priests held the ends of the sticks.

The priests took up the ark when Joshua bade them. They went to the edge of the water, not knowing what they were to do. They were dressed in white, and their feet were bare.

Joshua called to them, and desired them to stand still. Then he spoke to all the people. "Now," he said, "you will see a great wonder that God is going to do; when the priests put their feet in the water, a dry path shall be made."

All the people were come out of their tents, they had got all their things ready for their journey, and were looking at the priests.

Then Joshua desired the priests to put their feet into the water.

As soon as they touched it, the water stood up like a wall on each side, and there was a dry path made through the river. The priests walked along, till they came to the middle of the river; then they stopped, and Joshua said to the people, "Now do you pass over Jordan."

While the people were crossing, the priests stood

quite still in the middle of the river. At last, all the people had got over into the land of Canaan, except twelve men that Joshua had desired to stay on the other side.

Why had Joshua desired them to stay?

Joshua said to them, "See where the priests are standing: there are great stones lying near them; take up twelve great stones, and bring them over with you into Canaan." These twelve men walked through the dry path; each took up a great stone in his arms, and carried it to the other side. Then Joshua said to them, "Put the twelve stones by the side of the river in Canaan."

Why do you think the stones were to be put there?

It was that people might never forget this great wonder of making a path in Jordan. God knew, that a long time afterwards, little children would see the twelve stones, and would say to their fathers, "What are these stones for?"

Then their fathers would say, "These stones were once at the bottom of the water: but God made a path for us, and we have put the stones here, to keep God's kindness in our minds."

God is pleased that children should wish to know the meaning of what they see. God wishes little children to know about his goodness, and the wonders he has done.

All the time the twelve men were walking through with the stones, the priests were standing still in the river.

At last Joshua said to the priests, "Come up out of Jordan:" so the priests came up out of the river. As soon as the priests put their feet on the dry land in Canaan, the water rolled back again, and the river looked as it had done before.

How happy the Israelites must now have been. They had wandered forty years in the wilderness, but at last they were safely arrived in Canaan. God had been very good to them, and he would help them to fight against the wicked people of Canaan.

Why did God desire that the people in Canaan should be killed? Because they went on worshipping idols, and doing a great many wicked things, so God chose to punish them.

The king of Jericho saw the Israelites come over the river. He could look at them over his high walls. He was very much frightened, and so were all the people in Jericho. Only Rahab was not frightened: she knew she was safe: she believed in the true God.

The priests put down the ark; all the Israelites set up their tents, and waited outside Jericho. Rahab's red cord could be seen upon her window on the wall.

So the Israelites knew which was her house, and Joshua told them not to hurt the people who were in it.

The gates of Jericho were kept fast shut, that the Israelites might not get in: no one in Jericho went out, and no one came in, but every body kept inside the town.

Those wicked people would never again walk by the river side: the day of their death was very near. Ah! why did not they turn to God before it was too late?

My dear children, the day of judgment will come to us all at last. Now is the time to be sorry for our sins, and ask God for his Holy Spirit. If children will go on telling lies, quarrelling, and fighting, being bold and disobedient, they will come to a sad end.

But I hope, dear children, that you will love God, and that you will be saved.

The priests just dip their feet
  In Jordan's rapid stream:
The waters quick retreat
  Like walls of silver seem;
O! why do Jordan's waters fly,
And leave the stoney channel dry?

The priests in Jordan stay,
  While Israel's mighty host
With haste pursue their way
  To Canaan's pleasant coast.
What power restrains the flowing tide,
While in the deep the priests abide?

Full long the white rob'd band
  Wait in the depths below;
But when they reach the land,
  Once more the waters flow:
What hand has broke the unseen chain,
That did the waters' force restrain?

It is the Lord restrains
  The rapid river's tide;
It is the Lord unchains
  The walls on either side;
It is the Lord who thus would mark
His love to those who bear his ark.

CHILD.

O bless *me*, Lord, like those
  Who in the river stood;
A way for me unclose,
  Through this world's dangerous flood;
And lead me with thy numerous host
From lowest depths to heaven's high coast.*

CHAPTER XXXVIII.

JOSHUA, OR THE WALLS OF JERICHO.

Joshua v. 13—15. vi.

THE children of Israel had placed their tents all round the city of Jericho, but they waited till God told them what to do. They could not get through the strong gates, unless God helped them.

Joshua was the captain of the Israelites. He was a very brave man. He trusted in God to help him, and that made him brave.

I will now tell you a very wonderful thing that happened to Joshua while he was on the outside of Jericho.

* I will bring my people again from the depths of the sea.—Ps lxviii 22.

One day he looked up, and he saw a man standing before him a little way off. The man looked as if he was a soldier, and he held a sword in his hand. Joshua knew that this man was not one of the Israelites; but he could not tell who he was.

Joshua went up to the man and said, "Are you come to help us to fight? or are you come to help the people of Jericho?"

Then the man answered, "I am come as captain of the army of the Lord."

Now Joshua knew who this man was. Can you tell who he was?

He was greater than a man, greater than an angel. He was the Lord from heaven, even Jesus Christ.

Jesus did not become a little baby for a long while afterwards: but he always lived in heaven with his Father, and sometimes looked like a man, and came down upon the earth.*

Was it not very kind in the Lord Jesus to come down from heaven and to speak to Joshua?

When Joshua knew who the man was, he fell down with his face upon the ground, and worshipped him, saying, "What will my Lord say to his servant?"

Joshua called himself God's servant.

Then the great captain of God's army said,

* And the form of the fourth is like the Son of God.—Dan. iii. 25. Whose goings forth have been from of old, from everlasting.—Mic. v. 2

"Take your shoe off your foot, because this is holy ground."

Then Joshua took it off, and waited to know what the Lord would say to him.

Why was the ground holy? Because God was there. You know the priests wore no shoes when they walked in God's house.

The Lord told Joshua how he was to fight against Jericho.

Such a way of fighting was never known before. You shall soon hear what the Lord told Joshua to do.

When the Lord was gone back to heaven, Joshua called the priests, and all the people of Israel, and showed them what they must do. Joshua told some of the priests to take up the ark.

Then he called seven more priests, and said, "Each of you must take a ram's horn, and blow with it, like a trumpet, and walk before the ark.

(*You know that a ram is a sheep, and that it has crooked horns.*) Then Joshua called all the soldiers, and told them to go before the priests, and he told the rest of the people that had no swords or spears, (that is, the women and children,) to walk behind the priests.

Where were they all to walk? Joshua desired them to walk round the city of Jericho. The soldiers with their swords and spears went first; next came seven priests dressed in their white clothes, blowing with the rams' horns. Then came the priests carrying the ark, and behind them all the people that had no swords or spears.

You never saw such a great number of people walking along.

Before they set out, Joshua told them not to make any shoutings, but to wait till he said, "Shout."

What is shouting? Calling out loud. Soldiers shout when they have conquered. The Israelites were not to shout till Joshua told them.

They all walked once round Jericho.

The people of Jericho heard the trumpets blowing, and they saw the men with swords and spears.

I dare say they thought the Israelites were going to shoot their arrows over the walls, and try and beat down the walls. How much frightened they must have been! Rahab took care to keep in her house, with all her dear friends. The Israelites walked once round, and then Joshua brought them back to their tents.

Are you not surprised to hear this? What was the use of walking round? You will hear what happened in the end.

The next day, Joshua made the people and the priests walk round once more, and then brought them home. Then, next day after, they went round again; and the next day, and the next day. Six days, one after the other, they walked round Jericho, and came home to their tents again, without having fought.

The Israelites behaved well in doing as Joshua

told them, instead of asking why they must walk round without fighting.

Do you not think that the people of Jericho began to laugh at the Israelites, and to think that they would never get into the city?

At last, after six days, Joshua told the Israelites to get up very early in the morning, as soon as it was light. He told them to walk all round as before; but when they had walked round, he did not tell them to go back to their tents, but to walk round again. That day they walked round seven times: they spent the whole day in walking round and round the city of Jericho.

When they had just finished walking round the seventh time, Joshua said to the people, "Now, when the priests blow again with the trumpets, you may shout; for God has given you the city. You will soon get in; you must kill all the people except Rahab and her friends that are in her house; you will find many beautiful things in Jericho: but you must not keep anything to yourselves; but you must bring the cups of gold, and silver, and brass, and iron, to the Lord; and you must not keep anything for yourselves. Bring all you find to the house of the Lord; for God has cursed Jericho, and everything in it."

When Joshua had done speaking, the priests blew again with the trumpets, and the people gave a great shout. At the same moment, the walls of Jericho fell down. How horrible was the crash of those great walls! Now the men of Jericho saw that the day was come when they must die.

The two spies ran quickly to Rahab's house, and brought her out, and her father, and mother, and brothers, and sisters, and led them to a safe place near the tents of the Israelites. Rahab and her friends brought all their things with them out of the house: so they could make tents, and live together. O happy Rahab! Now she could learn more about the true God; she could see God's priests offering sacrifices on the altar, and could hear how her sins might be forgiven by the blood of Jesus, the Lamb of God, who would come into the world.

But what happened to the people in Jericho? They were all killed; the men, the women, and the children—even the sheep, and cows, and all the beasts, were killed; not one was left alive. The Israelites killed them with their swords. Then they set fire to the houses, and burnt them all up; but the cups and basins, made of gold, and silver, and brass, and iron, they brought to the priests for God's house. What would the priests do with the basins? They would put in them the blood of the sheep and goats that they sacrificed on the altar.

All the other people in Canaan heard about Jericho, and they were more frightened than before. They said, "What a great captain Joshua is!"

But you know who was the captain that fought for Joshua Who was it threw down the walls?

Was it not the man whom Joshua had seen. He was a captain over thousands of angels, that filled the air, and obeyed all he said. The angels are stronger than men; and Jesus is their captain, and he is God himself. He can break down walls, and he can build them up; he can kill, and he can make alive; he can shut us up in hell, and he can lift us up to heaven.

Which do you wish him to do for you, my dear children? Let us pray to him to save us when the world is burnt up; as he saved Rahab when Jericho was burnt up.

The trumpets seem to sound in vain;
For still the walls upright remain,
Can those within,
Who hear the din,
Once apprehend
How all will end?

The seventh time the priests walk round;
The walls no more resist the sound,
They totter now,
They crack, they bow:
Their sudden fall
All hearts appal.

Some take to arms, some flee away;
God is more swift and strong than they;
And vain is might,
And vain is flight;
For God pursues,
And all subdues.

CHILD.

A trump shall sound, ('twill be the last,)
And loud shall be that trumpet's blast;

The dead shall wake,
The mountains quake,
The sea shall roar,
The fire devour.

God yet prolongs the day of grace,
That all may turn, and seek his face.*
Still parents teach;
Still pastors preach;
And still I may
For mercy pray.

But should I this sweet season lose,
And God's repeated calls refuse,
I fear to think
Where I should sink
When that loud blast
Should sound at last.

CHAPTER XXXIX.

JOSHUA, HIS DEATH.

YOU have heard what the Israelites did to Jericho. There were a great many other cities in Canaan besides Jericho. The Israelites fought against the other cities of Canaan.

All the people in Canaan heard of it, and were much afraid of Joshua; but still they took their swords and spears, and fought against him.

* The Lord is not slack concerning his promise, as some men count slackness: but is long-suffering to us-ward: not willing that any should perish, but that *all* should come to repentance.—2 Peter iii. 9.

And who do you think conquered? God always helped the Israelites; so they always conquered. They went all through Canaan. First they went to one city, and killed the people in it; then they went to another city, and killed the people in it; so they went to hundreds of cities, till they had killed almost all the people in Canaan. God did not make the walls of the other cities to fall down, like the walls of Jericho; but the Israelites were obliged to fight very hard before they could get in.

At last Joshua said to the children of Israel, "Now the people of Canaan are dead, I will give you places to live in." So he gave to each of the Israelites a house, full of nice and beautiful things, and a garden, and a field, and a well of water.

Now the Israelites rested. They sat down under the fig-trees and vines in their own gardens, and ate the figs and grapes that grew on them, and they drank water out of the wells in their gardens.

Did the Israelites build their own houses? No; they lived in the houses of the people of Canaan. The wicked people had built the houses, and they had dug the wells, and planted the trees in the gardens:* but God had taken them away from these wicked people, and had given them to the Israelites.

Might God give them to whom he pleased? Yes: God made everything and everything be-

* To give thee great and goodly cities, which thou buildest not; houses full of good things, which thou filledst not; and wells digged, which thou diggedst not; vineyards and olive-trees, which thou plantedst not.—Deut. vi. 10, 11.

longs to God; and he may give things to whom he pleases. Sometimes he takes his things away from wicked people.

When the Israelites sat in their gardens, they ought to have thought to themselves, "How kind in God to give us so much! How much we ought to love him!" Has not God given you a great many things, my dear child? Ought not you to love him very much?

Why did God give so many things to the Israelites? Were the Israelites good? No; they were naughty. Then why was God so kind to them?

You remember the promise God had made to Abraham. God had said that he would give Canaan to his children's children. And did God keep his word? O yes! he remembered his promise, and he brought the Israelites into Canaan.* So the reason God was so kind to the Israelites was, because he had promised Abraham he would be kind to his children.

There was one thing which Joshua did not forget to do; that was to place the tabernacle in Canaan. He set it up in the middle of Canaan, at a place called Shiloh. Now the Israelites would not be obliged to move it about any more.

Joshua told them all to come up and worship God in the tabernacle; but some lived so far off that they could not come often. So they came only sometimes to the tabernacle.

* When the Lord thy God shall have brought thee into the land, which he sware unto thy fathers.—Deut. vi. 10.

God desired the Israelites not to worship the idols that the wicked people in Canaan had made. The Israelites would find their idols in the fields and gardens; and some of these idols were made of silver and gold; but the Israelites were not to keep them, even if they were pretty images: they were not to take the idols into their houses: but they were to burn them in the fire; because God hated these idols.*

At last Joshua grew very old; and he knew that he must die. So he called a great many of the Israelites together, that he might speak to them before he died.

Joshua stood near a great oak-tree while he spoke. He said to the Israelites, "I am soon going to die. Whom will you worship after I am dead? Will you worship idols, or will you worship God who has been so kind to you?"

Now which do you think the Israelites chose to worship? They all said, "We will worship God."

Then Joshua said, "If you choose to worship God, you must not worship idols too."

Then they answered "We will serve God."

"Now," said Joshua, "you have promised to serve God only. You must keep your promise."

Then Joshua took a book and wrote down what the people had said. Afterwards Joshua took a great stone, and put it under the oak, and said, "See this stone; I have put it here, to make you remember your promise always."

* Deut. vii. 25, 26.

Then Joshua told all the people to go home.

Very soon afterwards Joshua died. He was more than a hundred years old when he died.

Did the Israelites keep their promise? Did they worship idols, or did they not?

At first they did not worship idols. But at last they grew tired of serving God, and began to worship idols, and to do other wicked things.

My dear children, your parents have not taught you to worship idols, but you have done other naughty things. Have you never been disobedient, nor told lies, nor fallen into passions?

What can you do to please God?* Speak the truth, obey your parents, and be very kind to each other. These are things that please God.

Do you not wish to please God, who has been so kind to you, and has given you food, and clothes, and a house, and kind friends, and a body, and a soul, and who has even given his Son to die for you? Ask God to make you love him, and wish to please him.

The Israelites no more
  Dwell in the wilderness;
Their wanderings are o'er
  Blest Canaan they possess;
And, shaded from the heat,
  Beneath the spreading vine,
They eat the finest wheat,
  And drink the choicest wine.†

* Ye have received of us how ye ought to walk, and to please God. Thes. iv. 1.

† Amongst the provisions of Canaan is enumerated "the fat of the

The Lord could not forget
  How he did condescend,
His wondrous love to set
  On Abraham, his friend;†
And how he promised,
  That with a mighty hand
His children should be led
  To Canaan's pleasant land.†

And God has brought him there
  By his own arm alone;
O let them never dare
  To worship gods of stone.
If 'midst the thickest trees
  To idols they shall bend,
At length the Lord will cease
  His people to defend.

CHILD.

The Lord will bless me too,
  If I serve him alone,
His mercies, like the dew,
  Shall still be poured down;
But Satan stands by me,
  And seems an angel bright,‡
And promises that he
  Will fill me with delight.

kidneys of wheat:" and it is added, "thou didst drink the pure blood of the grape."—Deut. xxxii. 14.

* Because he loved thy fathers, therefore he chose their seed after them.—Deut. iv. 37.

† And he said unto Abraham, Know of a surety, that thy seed shall be a stranger in a land that is not theirs, and shall serve them. . . . . And also that nation whom they serve will I judge; and afterwards shall they come out with great substance.—Deut. xv. 13, 14.

‡ Satan himself is transformed into an angel of light.—1 Cor. xi. 14.

O, if I now attend
  To Satan's promise fair,
I shall to hell descend,
  And Satan's torments share.
My God deserves my love,
  And he deserves the whole;
Then to his house above
  He'll take my happy soul.

A FEW PRINCIPAL QUESTIONS

FOR THE EXAMINATION

Of Children who have finished reading this Book.

1. What promise did the Lord Jesus make to his Father a long while before Adam and Eve had sinned?
2. How used people to offer sacrifices?
3. Why did God desire people to offer sacrifices?
4. Why did Cain kill Abel?
5. Why did God drown the world?
6. Whom did God save when the world was drowned?
7. Whom did God desire to leave his own country, and go to a land that he would show him?
8. What land did God promise to give to Abraham's children's children?
9. What was the name of Abraham's son?
10. What were the names of Isaac's two sons?
11. How many sons had Jacob?
12. What cruel thing did Joseph's brothers do to him?
13. Why did the king of Egypt make Joseph a great lord?
14. How did Joseph save people from starving, when scarcely any corn grew in the fields?
15. Where did Joseph ask his brothers to come and live?
16. What was Jacob's other name?
17. Who were the Israelites?
18. Who desired the babies cf the Israelites to be drowned?
19. Who found Moses in the river, and called him her own son?
20. When Moses was grown up, where did he wish to take the Israelites?
21. Where did God desire Moses to go, when he spoke to him in the burning bush?

22. Why did God send ten plagues to king Pharaoh?

23. On the night that the eldest sons were killed, what did the Israelites eat, and what did they sprinkle on their doors?

24. What was the name of that supper?

25. How were Pharaoh and his servants killed?

26. How did the Israelites know which way to go to Canaan?

27. How were they fed in the wilderness?

28. What words did God speak very loud from Mount Sinai?

29. When Moses was alone with God on Mount Sinai, what did God desire him to make?

30. Who was to be the high priest?

31. What was the ark of God?

32. Why did the Israelites send twelve spies into Canaan?

33. Why did the Israelites say they would go back into Egypt?

34. What punishment did God give the Israelites for murmuring at what the spies had said?

35. Why ought the Israelites not to have been afraid of the strong men in Canaan?

36. How did Moses and Aaron offend God?

37. Whom did God desire to take care of the Israelites after Moses was dead?

38. What was the first city in Canaan that the Israelites conquered?

39. Why did God bring the Israelites into Canaan?

40. Why did God desire the Israelites to kill the people of Canaan?

QUESTIONS ON THE CHAPTERS.

I.

Why is God called the Creator?
Can men or angels create things?
What did God create on the first day?
On the second day?
On the third day?
On the fourth day?
On the fifth day?
On the sixth day?
What was the last thing God made?
What did God do on the seventh day?
Which of the creatures can praise God?

II.

Of what tree was Adam forbidden to eat?
Who asked Eve to eat of it?
Why did Eve eat some?
To whom did Eve give some of the fruit?
What punishment did God give to the serpent?
What punishment did he give to Eve?
What punishment did he give to Adam?
Why did not God allow Adam and Eve to stay in the garden of Eden?
What had the Son of God promised to his Father?

III.

What were the names of the two eldest sons of Adam and Eve?
Had Adam's children naughty hearts?

How did God make Abel good?
What used Cain to do?
What used Abel to do?
How did people offer sacrifices?
What was the heap of stones called, on which the lamb or kid was burnt?
Why did God desire people to offer sacrifices?
Why did God like Abel's sacrifice better than Cain s?
Why did Cain kill Abel?
How did Cain answer God when he asked him where Abel was?
What punishment did God give to Cain?
What was the name of Adam's youngest son?

IV.

Why did God determine to drown the world?
How was Noah saved?
Did God let the wicked people know that the world was soon to be drowned?
What birds did Noah send out of the ark to see whether the earth was dry?
What promise did God make Noah?
Of what should the rainbow make us think when we see it?

V.

Whom did most of the people in the world pray to?
Whom did God choose to be his servant and friend?
What was the name of Abraham's wife?
In what did Abraham sleep when he travelled?
To what land did God take Abraham?
What kind of people lived in Canaan?
Why was God pleased with Abraham?
What did God call him?
Might you be God's friend?

VI.

How many grandchildren and great-grandchildren did God promise to give Abraham?

Why did three angels come to Abraham's tent?

How did Abraham treat them?

How soon did they say that Abraham and Sarah should have a son?

Did Sarah believe at first?

Did God keep his promise?

What was the son's name?

Why was God pleased with Abraham?

VII.

Why did God tell Abraham to offer up his son as a sacrifice?

Would Abraham do as God told him?

What did Isaac say to his father as he walked up the hill?

What was it Abraham did when he was on the top of the hill?

How was Abraham hindered from killing Isaac?

Why ought we to love God better than every one else?

VIII.

Who buried Sarah?

Where was she buried?

Who was Isaac's wife?

What were the names of Isaac's children?

What were their employments?

Did they love God?

Why did Jacob leave his home and go to a country a great way off?

What dream did he have as he slept on the ground?

When Jacob woke what did he do? and what did he say to God?

IX.

Who was Rachel ?

Where did Jacob first see her ?

What was the name of Jacob's uncle ?

What did Jacob do for Laban ?

Who were Jacob's wives ?

Had Jacob any sheep and goats of his own ?

Why did Jacob wish to live in Canaan again ?

X.

Who told Jacob to go home to his father ?

What was Jacob afraid of when he was on his way home ?

What was it Jacob did when he was afraid ?

How did Esau behave to Jacob when he met him ?

Did Jacob ever go again to the place where he had seen the angels ?

What kind things had God done for Jacob since he had last been there ?

XI.

How many sons had Jacob ?

Which was the best ?

Which did Jacob love the best ?

Why did not Joseph's brothers love him ?

What did Jacob give to Joseph ?

What two dreams did Joseph have ?

Why did these dreams make the brothers angry with Joseph ?

Why did Jacob send Joseph to his brothers when they were keeping sheep ?

Where did the brothers throw him ?

XII.

Who passed by Joseph's brothers while they were eating near the pit ?

What did Judah advise the brothers to do with Joseph ?
For how much did they sell him ?
What did the brothers do with Joseph's coat ?
Why did they dip it in blood ?
What did Jacob think when he saw it ?
How do wicked people try to hide their faults ?

XIII.

Where was Joseph taken by the men who bought him of his brothrers ?
To whom did they sell Joseph ?
How did Potiphar treat Joseph ?
Who spoke against Joseph to Potiphar ?
How did Potiphar punish Joseph ?
How did the keeper treat Joseph ?

XIV.

What two men did Potiphar place under Joseph's care ?
What made them look sad one morning when Joseph came in ?
What was the butler's dream ?
What was the meaning of it ?
What was the baker's dream ?
What was the meaning of it ?
What was it Joseph asked the butler to do for him ?
Did the butler remember Joseph ?
What is it "to be ungrateful ?"
Who begs for us in heaven ?

XV.

What two dreams did Pharaoh king of Egypt have one night ?
Who advised him to send for Joseph ?
Why was Joseph able to tell him the meaning of the dreams ?
What was the meaning of the dreams ?

What did Joseph advise the king to do, to prevent the people from being starved when no corn should grow ?

Why did Pharaoh make Joseph ruler over the people ?

XVI.

When no corn grew in the fields, to whom did the people go for corn ?

Did Joseph know his brothers again when he saw them ?

Did they know him ?

Why did not they know him again ?

How did Joseph's dream about the sheaves come true ?

Why did Joseph speak unkindly to his brothers.

What did he say they were come to see ?

Where did he keep them for three days ?

Whom did Joseph desire them to bring with them the next time they came ?

Which of the brothers did Joseph keep in prison while the others went to fetch Benjamin ?

What did Joseph desire his servants to put into his brother's sacks with the corn ?

Why were the brothers frightened when they found the money in their sacks ?

Why would not Jacob let Benjamin go with his brothers to Egypt ?

XVII.

Who promised Jacob to take care of Benjamin, if Jacob would let him go into Egypt ?

What did Jacob advise his sons to take with them ?

When the brothers were come to Egypt, where did Joseph's servant bring them ?

Why were the brothers so much frightened ?

Who told them at last who had put the money in the sacks ?

When Joseph came into the house, how did the brothers show their respect for him ?

What did Joseph say when he saw Benjamin ?

Why did Joseph cry ?

Who sat at each of the three tables ?

To which of the brothers was Joseph the most kind ?

Were the brothers envious of Benjamin ?

Whom was Joseph like to, when he was kind to his unkind brothers ?

XVIII.

What did Joseph's servant ask the brothers whether they had stolen ?

What did the servant say should be done to that one who had stolen it ?

In whose sack was it found ?

Who had put it in Benjamin's sack ?

Did the servant allow Benjamin's brothers to go home to their father ?

Why did the brothers return to Joseph with Benjamin ?

Why was Joseph pleased to see that they came back with Benjamin ?

What did Judah ask Joseph to do, instead of keeping Benjamin ?

Why did Joseph *then* tell his brothers who he was ?

Why were they frightened at hearing he was Joseph ?

How did Joseph behave to them ?

XIX.

Whom did Pharaoh invite to live in Egypt ?

Why was not Jacob pleased when he first heard that Joseph was alive ?

What made Jacob believe at last that Joseph was alive ?

How did the little children make such a long journey into Egypt ?

Who met Jacob on his coming into Egypt ?

To whom did Joseph show his old father ?

How did Pharaoh behave to Jacob ?

Where did Jacob and his sons live?

Where did Jacob desire his sons to bury him?

What were the brothers afraid of after Jacob was dead?

Was Joseph as kind after Jacob's death as he had been before?

What was the name of Joseph's father?

And of Jacob's father?

And of Isaac's father?

What was the name of Abraham's wife?

Of Isaac's wife?

Of Jacob's wives?

How many sons had Jacob?

What promises had God make to Abraham, Isaac, and Jacob?

XX.

What was Jacob's other name?

What name was given to all the children, and grandchildren, and great-grandchildren of Jacob?

When the Pharaoh, who loved Joseph, was dead, who was the king of Egypt?

Why did that Pharaoh make the children of Israel work so very hard in making bricks?

What did he desire to be done to the boy-babies of the children of Israel?

What was it that one of the women did with her baby?

When she could no longer hide it, where did she put it?

Who watched to see what would become of the baby?

Who found the baby?

What did the princess call it?

Whom did she hire to be his nurse?

Whose son was Moses called?

Was Moses rich and great?

What promise had God made to Abraham about his children's children?

XXI.

When Moses was grown up, where did he go?

Where did Moses wish to lead the children of Israel?

What did Moses find them doing?

Who were the taskmasters?

What did Moses do to one of these cruel men?

Was it right in Moses to kill him?

Did anybody see Moses kill him?

Why did Moses go into a country a great way off?

What might Moses have been if he had chosen it?

Why did he choose rather to help the children of Israel?

Who once left his throne in heaven to save us from Satan?

XXII.

When Moses ran away from Egypt, where did he at length rest himself?

What kindness did Moses show to seven girls?

What kindness did their father show to him?

How used Moses employ himself?

What wonderful sight did he see while he was leading his sheep?

Where did God tell Moses to go?

Why did God determine to bring the children of Israel into Canaan?

What two wonderful things did God make Moses able to do?

Why did God make Moses able to do those wonderful things?

Who did God tell Moses should speak for him when he got to Egypt?

When Moses and Aaron were come to Egypt, what did they say to the children of Israel?

Did the Israelites believe that God had really spoken to Moses?

Did the children of Israel wish to go to Canaan?

XXIII.

When Moses and Aaron asked Pharaoh to let Israel go to Canaan, what did Pharaoh answer?

What was the first thing Moses and Aaron did to show Pharaoh that God had sent them?

Why did God turn the water into blood?

Repeat the six plagues I have told you of.

XXIV.

When the dreadful storm came, how did some people escape being hurt?

What are locusts?

When the three days' darkness came, where was it light?

When Pharaoh wished the plagues to be taken away, who asked God to take them away?

What was the last plague?

Why did the Israelites mark their doors with blood?

What were they doing when Pharaoh sent them away?

Why did God desire the Israelites to eat a lamb in the night every year?

What was that supper called?

Why was it called the Passover?

Why was the lamb of the Passover like Jesus?

Can you repeat the ten plagues?

Is there any place where there are worse plagues than those ten plagues?

XXV.

How did the Israelites know which was the way to Canaan?

Who tried to overtake the Israelites after they had left Egypt?

How did they cross the Red Sea?

Why could the Israelites see their way clearly in the night?

Why could not Pharaoh and his men see well also?

Why were Pharaoh and his men frightened when they were in the middle of the sea?

What became of Pharaoh and his men?

What did the sea toss up the next morning on the side of the sea where the Israelites were?

How did the Israelites show that they were thankful to God for saving them?

Who wishes to keep our souls from going to heaven?

XXVI.

What sort of a place was the wilderness?

How did the Israelites behave when they had nothing to eat?

How did God feed them?

Why were the Israelites obliged to pick up the manna very early?

What became of the manna if it was kept to the next day?

How did the Israelites behave when they had nothing to drink?

How did God give them water?

XXVII.

Whom did God desire to come up the mountain, that he might speak to him?

Why were rails put round the mountain?

What was seen upon the mountain when God came down upon it?

What words did the people hear God speak in a very loud voice?

Why did the people wish never to hear that voice again?

How long did Moses stay on the top of the mountain, alone with God?

What did God give to Moses when he had done talking with him?

What did the Israelites do when they were tired of waiting for Moses?

Who made the calf?

Who told Moses what the Israelites were doing?

Who begged God not to kill them?

Why did Moses throw down the tables of stone?

What did Moses do with the calf?

What did he desire some of the people to do with their swords?

Did God give the people any other punishment?

When Moses stayed with God on the mountain forty days more, what glorious sight did God show him?

Why were the Israelites afraid to come near him when he came down again?

Why was his face bright?

When do you hope to shine, as Moses did?

XXIX.

When Moses was on the top of the mountain, what did God tell Moses to make?

What did the Israelites give to Moses to make the house of?

How did two men know how to make so beautiful a house?

Why was not this house fastened to the ground?

What was this house called?

What were the walls of the house made of?

What was thrown over the top of the house?

What kind of a door was there?

How many rooms were there in the tabernacle?

Tell me three things in the first room.

What was burnt on the golden altar?

What was placed on the golden table?

How many lamps were there in the candlestick?

What was the little room called?

What was there in it?

What was inside the ark?

What was the top of the ark called?

Where did the cloud of God sit in this little room?

What made this room light?
What made the other room light?
What makes heaven light?

XXX.

What was placed round the court of the tabernacle?
What two things were placed in the court?
What was to be burned upon the altar of brass?
Who was to wash in the brass basin?
Who was to be high priest?
Where might the high priest go only once a year?
What clothes was Aaron to wear?
What was to be written on Aaron's mitre?
Who was to help Aaron to offer sacrifices?
What sort of clothes were they to wear?
Who set up the tabernacle?
On what did Moses pour oil?
What was this pouring of oil called?
What was seen upon the tabernacle after it was set up?
Why ought the Israelites to have been very happy?

XXXI.

What sacrifice was offered every morning and every evening on the brass altar?
What was it the priests never let go out?
Who ate the shew bread when it was taken from the golden table?
Who might go into the tabernacle?
Who is our high priest?
What is he doing for us in heaven?
When did the priests blow the silver trumpets?
Who carried the ark?
What sweet land do we hope to reach?

XXXII.

Why did Moses send twelve men into Canaan?

What did these men bring back with them?

What sort of a land did the spies say that Canaan was?

What sort of people did the spies say lived in Canaan?

What were the names of the two good spies?

Why ought not the Israelites to have been afraid of the people of Canaan?

What was Moses doing when God spoke to him from the tabernacle?

How did God say that he would punish the Israelites for their wickedness?

Would the little children die in the wilderness?

Would any of the grown-up people be allowed to go into Canaan?

How many years would it be before the Israelites would go into Canaan?

XXXIII.

How did the people behave when they had no water to drink?

How did God desire Moses to bring water out of the rock?

What was it Moses did instead of speaking to the rock?

What did Moses and Aaron say as they stood by the rock?

How did God say that he would punish them?

Was Moses often angry?

Was Moses meek?

How would a meek child behave if he were ill treated?

Who went with Aaron to the top of the hill when he was to die?

What clothes did Aaron wear?

Upon whom did Moses put the clothes just before Aaron died?

Why did Moses put the clothes on Aaron's son?

Who was the high priest when Aaron was dead?

XXXIV.

How did the Israelites behave when God made them stay a long while in the wilderness?

What living creatures did God send to punish them?

What did God desire Moses to do, to cure the people who were bitten?

Who has made our souls ready to die?

When did Satan first make people's souls naughty?

At whom must we look that our souls may live?

Are we to look at Jesus with the eyes of our body?

What do you mean by "looking at Jesus?"

XXXV.

What *did* Moses write down in five books?

How did Moses know what to write?

Whom did Moses desire to read his books to the children of Israel?

Who was to take charge of the people when Moses was dead?

Why did God desire Moses to go up to the top of a high mountain before he died?

Who buried Moses?

How used God to talk to Moses?

If you are like Moses, what shall you like doing when you are grown up?

XXXVI.

What city did the Israelites see on the other side of the river?

Why did Joshua send two spies to Jericho?

To whose house did they go?

Who sent to Rahab's house to look for them?

Where had Rahab hid them?

What promise did Rahab ask the spies to make her?

How did the spies come out of Jericho?

Why did they desire Rahab to bind the red rope to her window?

In what way do you hope God will save you?

XXXVII.

What would the Israelites have to cross before they could get into Canaan ?

What did Joshua desire the priests to do ?

What happened when the priests put their feet into the river Jordan ?

Where did the priests stop while the people were crossing the river ?

Why did Joshua desire twelve men to take up twelve stones from the river, and to place them in Canaan ?

When did the water of the river cover up the dry path again ?

How long had the Israelites been travelling through the wilderness ?

Who were the only persons in Jericho whom God meant to save ?

Why did God desire the Israelites to kill the other people in Jericho ?

XXXVIII.

Who was the man with a sword that Joshua saw near Jericho ?

Who told Joshua how to conquer Jericho ?

Who was to blow the ram's horns ?

How many days did the Israelites walk round Jericho ?

How many times did they walk round on the seventh day ?

What did the *people* do *just* before the walls fell down ?

What did the priests do *just* before the walls fell down ?

What became of the people of Jericho ?

What became of the city of Jericho ?

What day does the burning of Jericho make you think of ?

XXXIX.

What did Joshua give to the Israelites after the people in Canaan were killed ?

Why did God give so much to the Israelites?

Why did God desire the Israelites to kill the people in Canaan?

Where did Joshua place the tabernacle?

What had God desired the Israelites to do with the wicked people's idols?

What question did Joshua ask the Israelites before he died?

What promise did the Israelites make to Joshua?

Why did Joshua place a stone under the oak-tree?

Why ought we to love God, and to try and please him?

VERSES OF SCRIPTURE.

THE following verses are applicable to the preceding lessons, and one of them may be learned by heart after each lesson has been taught to the little pupils.

The titles prefixed may be useful in reminding the children of the subjects of the verses.

It is recommended that the pupils should not be required to name the parts of scripture whence the verses are taken.

---

1. *How long God was in making the world.*

In six days the Lord made heaven and earth, the sea, and all that in them is, and rested the seventh day.—Ex. xx. 11.

2. *Who are the devil's children.*

He that committeth sin is of the devil; for the devil sinneth from the beginning.—1 John iii. 16.

3. *About Cain.*

Cain was of that wicked one, and slew his brother. 1 John iii. 12.

4. *About the flood.*

(God) spared not the old world, but saved Noah, the eighth person, a preacher of righteousness, bringing in the flood upon the world of the ungodly.—2 Peter ii. 5.

5. *Who are God's friends.*

Ye are my friends, if ye do whatsoever I command you. —John xv. 14.

6. *How Abraham pleased God.*

(Abraham) believed in the Lord; and he counted it to him for righteousness.—Gen. xv. 6.

7. *Who loves God?*

He that hath my commandments, and keepeth them, he it is that loveth me.—John xiv. 21.

8. *How safe the righteous are.*

The eyes of the Lord are over the righteous, and his ears are open unto their prayers.—1 Peter iii. 12.

9. *How happy the righteous are.*

Blessed is every one that feareth the Lord; that walketh in his ways.—Ps. cxxviii. 1.

10. *Jacob's thanks to God for keeping his kind promise.*

I am not worthy of the least of all the mercies, and of all the truth, which thou hast showed unto thy servant.—Gen. xxxii. 10.

11. *What a wicked man thinks when he is doing wickedness.*

He hath said in his heart, "God hath forgotten: he hideth his face; he will never see it."—Ps. x. 11.

12. *How God will punish liars.*

All liars shall have their part in the lake which burneth with fire and brimstone.—Rev. xxi. 8.

13. *What the Lord promises to do for the righteous.*

I will be with him in trouble: I will deliver him and honour him.—Ps. xci. 15

14. *The Lord likes men to be patient.*

The Lord is good unto them that wait for him, to the soul that seeketh him.—Lam. iii. 25.

15. *Who is it that makes all things happen?*

The Lord maketh poor and maketh rich: he bringeth low and lifteth up.—1 Sam. ii. 7.

16. *How God saves the righteous and punishes the wicked.*

The righteous is delivered out of trouble, and the wicked cometh in his stead.—Prov. xi. 8.

17. *About forgiving others.*

If any man have a quarrel against any; as Christ forgave you, so also do ye.—Col. iii. 13.

18. *About the kindness of the Lord.*

Thou, Lord, art good and ready to forgive; and plenteous in mercy unto all them that call upon thee.—Ps. lxxxvi. 5.

19. *How the young should behave to the old.*

Thou shalt rise up before the hoary head, and honour the face of the old man, and fear thy God.—Lev. xix. 32

20. *What the righteous man does in his trouble.*

As for me I will call upon God, and the Lord shall save me.—Ps. lv. 16.

21. *The choice of the righteous.*

I had rather be a doorkeeper in the house of my God, than dwell in the tents of wickedness.—Ps. lxxxiv. 10.

22. *Why God sent Moses to bring the children of Israel out of Egypt.*

He remembered his holy promise, and Abraham his servant.—Ps. cv. 42.

23. *Whom we should fear.*

Thou, even thou, art to be feared; and who may stand in thy sight when once thou art angry?—Ps. lxxvi. 7.

24. *How terrible God is to the wicked.*

It is a fearful thing to fall into the hands of the living God.—Heb. x. 31.

25. *How God destroyed Pharaoh and his servants.*

Thou didst blow with thy wind, the sea covered them: they sank as lead in the mighty waters.—Ex. xv. 10.

26. *How God relieved the thirsty Israelites.*

He clave the rocks in the wilderness, and gave them drink as out of the great depths.—Ps. lxxviii. 15.

27. *What God wished the Israelites to do.*

O that there were such a heart in them, that they would fear me, and keep all my commandments always!—Deut v. 29.

28. *How the Israelites behaved to God.*

They forgat God their Saviour, which had done great things in Egypt.—Ps. cvi. 21.

29. *About the glorious light of heaven.*

And there shall be no light there; and they need no candle, neither light of the sun; for the Lord God giveth them light.—Rev. xxii. 5.

30. *Where God promised to dwell.*

I will dwell among the children of Israel, and will be their God.—Exod. xxix. 45.

31. *About the Lamb who died for us.*

Behold the lamb of God which taketh away the sin of the world.—John i. 29.

32. *How the Israelites behaved when the spies came back from viewing the land.*

They despised the pleasant land, they believed not (God's) word: but murmured in their tents, and hearkened not unto the voice of the Lord.—Ps. cvi. 24, 25.

33. *A prayer to be kept from sinful words.*

Set a watch, O Lord, before my mouth; keep the door of my lips.—Ps. cxli. 3.

34. *Why the serpent of brass was like Christ.*

And as Moses lifted up the serpent in the wilderness, even so must the Son of Man be lifted up: that whosoever believeth in him should not perish, but have eternal life.—John iii. 14, 15.

35. *How God shows his love when people sin.*

As many as I love, I rebuke and chasten.—Rev. iii. 19.

36. *What we must now do, if we hope to be saved in the judgment-day.*

Seek righteousness, seek meekness: it may be, ye shall be hid in the day of the Lord's anger.—Zeph. ii. 3.

37. *When we ought to seek for mercy from God.*

Seek ye the Lord while he may be found; call ye upon him while he is near.—Isa. lv. 6.

38. *What shall become at last of the wicked.*

Let sinners be consumed out of the earth, and let the wicked be no more.—Ps. civ. 35.

39. *Praise to God for his goodness.*

Bless the Lord, O my soul, and forget not all his benefits: who forgiveth all thine iniquities, who healeth all thy diseases.—Ps. ciii. 2, 3.

UNIVERSITY OF MICHIGAN
3 9015 02779 2293

PICTURE CARDS
BIBLE HISTORY

www.ingramcontent.com/pod-product-compliance
Lightning Source LLC
LaVergne TN
LVHW010245110826
845151LV00004B/1395

* 9 7 8 1 4 2 5 5 2 2 9 5 7 *